Jonny M(
Antrim, N
completir
politics at Queen's University,
worked in the NI media industry for
almost two decades, holding a number
of senior editorial positions, including
Deputy Editor at the *Belfast Telegraph*.
In 2016, Jonny gave up daily newspaper
journalism to concentrate on looking after his son. In 2017 he
launched the popular blog, *What's a Daddy For?* In 2020, he was
appointed News Editor of the *News Letter*.

Jonny currently lives in Hillsborough with his wife, Debs, also a
journalist, and their seven-year-old son, James.

Praise for *Afraid of the Dark*

'Packed with humour, wisdom and pathos, this is a compellingly
personal memoir by one of Northern Ireland's finest writers.

With effortless elegance, the author explores his own
remarkable story and with searing honesty questions some of
the assumptions by which many of us live our lives.

This book about a topic of deadly seriousness could have been
heavy, but it is always alive to the comic potential of even the
bleakest situation.'
Sam McBride, News Letter Political Editor, author of *Burned*

'Written by a gifted and courageous writer, this is a book every
home should have.'
Frank Mitchell, broadcaster and journalist

'. . . this book will cement Jonny McCambridge's second career – not just as a truth-telling journalist, but as an author of the highest ability, integrity, penmanship and – I am certain – literary success.'
Peter Cardwell, former UK government adviser, author of *The Secret Life of Special Advisers* and mental health patient

'Jonny McCambridge takes on his inner and outer demons with a cracking combination of grace, good humour, compassion, courage, love, self-deprecation and searing honesty. And brilliant writing. This is a wonderfully uplifting book.'
Alex Kane, writer and commentator

'Jonny's story redefined the meaning of the word 'courage' for me. *Afraid of the Dark* is one of the rawest, most poignant accounts I have ever read about one man's brutally honest battle with depression, self-worthlessness, and the daily struggles he faced with his mental health to prevent him from ending his own life.

It took courage to write this memoir. . . The shortcomings and unexpected challenges of life that test the already questionable reliability and resilience of our mental health often push us to the very limit of our ability to survive, forcing us in our darkest moments to ask that question, 'Is this life of mine really worth saving?' *Afraid of the Dark* reminded me beyond any doubt why the answer to this question is a resounding Yes.'
Gareth O'Callaghan, Writer and Broadcaster

Afraid of the Dark

Jonny McCambridge

Dalzell Press

First published in 2021 by Dalzell Press

Dalzell Press
54 Abbey Street
Bangor, N. Ireland
BT20 4JB

Supported by the National Lottery though the Arts
Council of Northern Ireland

LOTTERY FUNDED

To Debs and James – my wee family

Part One

One

The Dark

The room is small, softly lit. A smell of damp, like wet cardboard. A nurse arrives and sits opposite me. I can tell she is concerned that I might be trouble. It's the middle of the night. She's on the graveyard shift and doesn't need the agitation. But soon she relaxes a bit, probably sensing that I'm more afraid than angry. She smiles and puts her hand on top of mine for just a moment. The smallest gestures are often the ones which stay with you the longest.

'Well, sonny,' she begins in a rolling Scottish lilt. She's not much older than me, probably early 40s. Short and slight, but with an air of strength which belies her stature. 'How did ye end up in here?'

I shrug, trying to avoid her gaze. She has a kind, patient face which seems to say, 'No matter what you tell me, I've heard ten times worse before.' I don't speak, so she goes on.

'What do ye do for a living, son?'

I gather myself, trying desperately to find the person I know that I am. I summon some of my old authority, speaking more from habit than conviction.

'I'm a journalist. I'm News Editor at Northern Ireland's biggest newspaper.'

Her smile hasn't shifted and the eyes are steady and sympathetic. She leans forward and pats me on the arm.

'That's nice, sonny. That's nice...'

She leaves me alone in the room for just a minute. Then she returns, smiles again and tells me that she expects I'll be here for just a few days. It'll be like a short break. It sounds like something you tell someone in a bad situation to make them feel better. Neither of us really believes it. I'm taken to another room, this one with a bed, and told to relax, to try to get some sleep.

My wife is at home, picking up some of my personal things and I'm alone now. The bed is hard. I'm utterly exhausted but never has sleep seemed so far away. I lie there, terrified. How can I find a way back to any sort of life from this?

Soon, a man in a blue uniform comes into the room. Softly, he walks to the side of the bed and shines a torch into my eyes. At first, I'm confused, but then the awful realisation hits me. He's checking to make sure I'm still alive. I am on suicide watch. I shiver and pull the thin blanket closer around me, but it gives no warmth. I have to get used to it. I am in Ward 12. For now, this is my home.

I lie like this for hours. I watch the clock on the wall. The second hand never tires, yet never goes fast enough.

It feels like I've been watching the clock for so much of my life. It's my thing. I used to do it endlessly in school; at work; at home; on holiday. And like so much of the workings of my mind, there's not another person on this earth who knows anything about it. It's a technique. Not one I've been taught, but something I've developed myself over the years. I count the hours down, the minutes, the seconds. Constantly counting them down until another day is over. I suppose the idea is that when I'm thinking about time, I can't think about anything else. No two things can occupy the same space. It's a way of keeping me from the worst excesses of myself, the thoughts that terrify me.

I also have a phrase. Something I've been saying for years. Over and over, under my breath. 'Just let me get through this day. . . Just let me get through this day.' It's a false comfort, a trick played on my own brain. The next day is seldom better, usually worse, and the nights are the worst of all. That's when the fear is most intense, the edges of doubt are at their sharpest. You pray for sleep. Sometimes it comes, sometimes it doesn't.

So I watch the clock. There's some consolation in knowing that every day, no matter how black, can't outlast the clock. I need that comfort more than ever now. I'm in a strange place, a place I could never have imagined I would end up in. I always assumed I'd be dead before I'd see the corridors of this kind of hospital ward. The room is as desperate as I am. Paint peeling off the walls, tattered fading curtains, pillows limp and flat like burst balloons. A forgotten room for forgotten people.

***

It is much later. The early morning sun is beginning to creep across the floor. I rise from the bed before I realise that I don't know what I'm supposed to do next. So I just wander through the wards. There's a doctor who wants to talk to me, then another one. I won't open up to them. A nurse takes blood from my arm and gives me some tablets. Little white pills.

And then again, I walk. I go to the door which leads back to the outside world. It's locked. You need a code to leave and I don't have it. I'm a prisoner here. For the first time in my adult life, I don't have the right to come and go as I please. I need a signature on a piece of paper to leave this place. So I walk to the other side of the ward. There are other people up and down the corridor but I barely register them. There's a little room at the end with a couple of bookshelves, almost like a conservatory. It's empty. I decide this will be my place. I sit in the armchair and wait. I don't know what I'm waiting for or how long it will take. I watch the clock. I watch the raindrops on the window. A fat drop explodes on the glass and then runs down the pane like a tear. Like a tear.

I have so many emotions now. But most of all I'm angry. Angry at myself, for not holding it together. Angry at others, for putting me in here. Angry at my cowardice, that I allowed this to happen.

Soon yet another nurse comes to speak to me – it's an induction of sorts, a welcoming chat. She tells me about all the things they do here, as if it were a holiday camp. But I don't listen; I've no intention of taking part in any of their activities. I just sit here, watching the clock and the rain, and waiting for something to happen.

Eventually I get hungry. I've been sitting in the same spot for hours. I find my way to a canteen which smells of burnt fat. I choose a quiet corner. I don't even lift my head to see who else is about. Then something does actually happen. A large man with black hair and a red, round nose sits opposite me. One by one a few other men drift to the table. I look up, unsure what's going on. Then the large man holds out a giant hand, more like a paw. He has watery, kind eyes. I don't think I've offered my hand, but he takes it anyway. He tells me his name and introduces a few of the other patients. He asks my name.

'Uh, I'm Jonny.'

'We're all very pleased to meet you, Jonny. The first day's the worst, but we all stick together, and we'll help you get through it ok.'

But it's not fear I'm feeling now, it's deep shame. I had completely dehumanised these people, assumed I was too good to be in here with them. But the same rules of kindness and compassion apply inside this place as outside. I learn that just because you're damaged, it doesn't mean you still can't do a good thing, still try to help someone else. It all gets a little bit easier from here, just a little bit. The hours begin to turn like a slowly spinning wheel.

***

I'm kept in the single room by myself for just a couple of nights before I'm moved into a larger, even more dilapidated area. At first, I think this must be progress. There are four beds in this new room. One is empty. Otherwise, there are two younger men and me. Curtains, so thin you can see right through them, separate the beds. In the far corner is a scrawny boy with long ginger hair. He's probably in his early 20s and he cries all the time. Right through the night, behind his little curtain, the sobs never stop. Often, I hear him on the phone. He's whispering, but there are no secrets in here.

'Mum, please get me out of here. Please, Mum, I swear I won't do anything. Please, Mum, please. . . '

It's the most desperate and heartbreaking sound I've ever heard.

Our other roommate is even younger, I guess barely out of his teens, if at all. He rarely makes a sound. He is short and stocky, scars on his arms. His hair is coal-black and his eyes are too. I don't think I've ever looked into eyes like this before: eyes in which you can't see anything. When he walks his feet never seem to leave the ground, it's more of a shuffle than a walk and his slippers squeak against the floor.

On my first night in the room, I'm awoken by him thumping a shoe against the window. It's not an escape attempt, he's just doing it. Some medics calm him down and bring him back to his bed, less than six feet from mine. I lie there and feel the beginnings of yet another panic attack coming on. The sweating, the racing heart, the uncontrollable, disturbing thoughts. I don't want to be here; I don't want to be back outside either. My face is at the very edge of the pillow and I'm gripping the thin blanket so tight that my nails dig into my palms through its material. Spasms of despair are rising out of my stomach and I fight to push them back down. I don't understand how this place is supposed to be helping me.

There are perhaps 20 patients on the ward. It's mostly men, but there are a couple of females who join us in the communal areas during the day – they sleep in their own side room at night. There's one woman who walks up and down the corridor all day in her slippers. That's all she does, walking up and down. She never looks at me. Some of the patients are like me, just in for a few days, for a rest. But there are also those who've been here for a long time.

There's one elderly gentleman, smartly dressed. He always wears a tie. I get the impression that he hasn't left this ward in years; that it's become his protection against a scary world. During my stay, he is told that he is to be moved to a geriatric ward. He falls to pieces. We're in the canteen when we hear his wails. We move to see what is happening and catch a glimpse of him trying to run, being held and comforted by a nurse. His clothes are pulled and dishevelled. His face is purple, glistening with tears and imprinted with the kind of fear I've never witnessed before. It's the first time I've seen his tie not straight.

There are lots of activities on the ward. I guess they're supposed to heal us, but really, they're just a way to pass the time. We do 'relaxation'. Sitting in a room, listening to soothing music while a woman reads slowly to us in a mellifluous voice. We play games – word association games, games with cards. We're given writing tasks. Sometimes they allow us outside for a walk to the local garage to buy sweets or cigarettes. Accompanied, of course.

On one afternoon I am recruited onto a team for a 'concentration class' to be given by the occupational therapist, the 'OT'. I'm paired with a young man with untidy black hair and stubble that doesn't quite succeed in making him look grown-up. He tells me his name is Niall. He seems permanently afraid. We sit at a table opposite two other men, with the therapist at the side. She starts to talk as she lays large cards on the table. I can't follow her thread but I catch the terms 'cognitive dysfunction' and 'remediation activities'.

Then I hear her say, 'And guys, today we have with us, Jonny. Jonny is a very successful journalist. This should be right up your street, Jonny, because it's all about words. It should be very easy for a man of letters like yourself.'

I nod and smile weakly. Our opponents across the table are staring at me now, like boxers eyeing an opponent at a weigh-in. I notice that beside me, Niall's arm is trembling under the table. The game begins. The OT turns over a card which reveals a letter. We then have to shout out the name of an animal which begins with that letter. My reactions are slow – it feels like my thoughts are wading through treacle. And the other team are good, and very fast. It occurs to me they've probably played this a few times and have memorised a bank of animal names for each letter. Within minutes Niall and I are being soundly beaten. It's embarrassingly one-sided.

'Vulture. . . giraffe . . . ostrich. . . lemur. . . walrus!'

Eventually my brain reconciles itself to the game and I start to come up with a few answers. But for every one I name, our opponents are scoring at least three. Niall has not spoken but I can see his body moving back and forward as if he is physically trying to force his mind to find an answer. The therapist turns over another card. It's a 'K'. Niall leans forward anxiously, almost falling from his chair and shouts, 'Carrots!' Then he apologises and starts to chew on the collar of his shirt.

The therapist smiles at him. 'That's a really good try Niall,' she says.

The next card is a B, but Niall does the same thing again, yelling, 'Carrots!' One of the members of the other team says that he shouldn't be allowed to play but the OT pretends not to hear. I notice that the tremble in Niall's hand has developed into a shake. I reach under the table and give his hand a small squeeze inside mine. When I go to remove my hand, Niall hangs on. So we stay like that, trying to name animals and holding hands under the table.

We move on to another game. This time, the cards show animals and we have to come up with an adjective which starts with the same letter. The 'menacing monkey'. The 'crestfallen cow'. The other team are clearly familiar with this game too and begin rolling out phrases automatically, while my mind is floundering. Niall is no longer even trying to take part but seems to want to just be there as support for me. Now I feel a kind of desperation to get some good answers. I have to do it for Niall. The therapist turns over a card which shows an image of an octopus.

'The olygormythic octopus!' I yell immediately.

The OT gives me a confused look but I just nod knowingly. She's unsure but doesn't want to be seen to get it wrong. 'Ok Jonny, very good.'

The other team are about to protest but she turns over another card. This one reveals what might be a panther. 'The polycontabulistic panther!' I offer brightly.

This brings the game to the edge of chaos, with the other team threatening to go off in search of a dictionary. The OT decides it's better to stop the game now. Niall is rocking in his chair again but this time it's from pleasure. I notice he's mumbling softly, so that only I can hear.

'We won. . . we won. . . we won. . !'

***

The next day, the Friday, they throw a little party. The staff put buns and sausage rolls on paper plates and set them out on a long table in the canteen. A startlingly handsome woman with a guitar arrives from the outside world to sing to us. We gather in a circle around her and it begins. She strums and floats out a song about a train. She sings a bit and then we have to respond.

'And the train just keeps rolling on!'

This goes on. Some are too timid to do much more than mouth the words, others throw themselves into it with energy. I think I'm in the latter group.

'And the train just keeps rolling on!'

Then we're given instruments and we have to form a little orchestra. I've got a wooden stick which rattles when shaken. She plays another song, and we rattle and shake along to it. One of the patients, beside me, bursts into tears and is taken back to his bed. Then my phone rings and I

17

quickly answer without thinking, so as not to interrupt the song. It's a friend of mine, one of Northern Ireland's best-known journalists, calling to discuss a story. I've forgotten that there's an outside world, a world of work. I've forgotten nobody knows I'm in here.

'Uh, is everything ok, Jonny?' He must be able to hear the music and I can sense the confusion in his voice.

'Yeah, it's a bit difficult to talk right now, mate. I'm going to have to get back to you.'

Soon the music finishes. Some of the patients move off to eat the buns but a few of us stay behind. Our music teacher chats to us. Then she gets us to sit in a circle on the floor and we play a new game. It's a rhythm game, which involves clapping our hands and hitting a plastic cup off the floor so it makes a clicking sound. It's hypnotic and pleasing. It seems like we could play this game for a very long time.

Later, I help the nurses to clean up. Then I sit on a long windowsill and watch the heavy orange sun begin to sink. It's still September but I sense that the wind already contains the first harsh hint of winter; the leaves are starting to turn brown and crisp at the edges. Some of them have already fallen and are blowing around a small, paved yard where a few of the patients are now gathering for a smoke. One of the younger nurses comes to talk to me. She must gain comfort from the conversation because she shows me pictures of her two little girls, her face opening with pride. Suddenly I'm surprised by the late hour and realise I haven't looked at the clock all day.

Later that evening I meet my assigned psychiatrist. He's serious, scholarly and sympathetic all at once. He's keen to get me home, but also cautious. It's not that he thinks I'm better, more that he has to consider what the best environment for me to heal might be. He orders me to not even think about work, not for a long time. He then tells me he has also spoken to my wife, who is waiting on the other side of the wall. It's not just about me; he needs to know that Debs is comfortable with having me back at the house. I'm almost afraid to get my hopes up as he reads endless reports and scratches his nose.

All at once with a flourish, he signs a form – and just like that, I'm free again. I quickly pack my bag and say goodbye to some of the staff and patients. I let the handshakes linger as I've no idea if I'll ever see these people again. As I travel down in the lift, I can't bear to let go of my wife's hand; I don't want to let go of it ever again.

But as we walk out into the carpark, there's a familiar feeling. A little bit of anxiety begins to return. The truth is, there's a dangerous comfort in being inside, in not having any responsibility, in letting someone else make all the decisions. But, of course, that's not real life. As I get into the car, my thoughts are racing again, persistent and demanding. The weight of knowing that people depend on me – family members and work colleagues – is coming back.

And there's another person to consider, the other main player in this story, who hasn't yet been mentioned – our infant son, James, who is asleep at home, oblivious to all of his daddy's failures and weaknesses. Just four months old. I think about how I'm going to hold him in my arms, bury my face in his neck, feel his warmth, smell him. Our wonderful, astonishing, beautiful boy. But I also think about his helplessness and I'm troubled by a familiar, half-formed thought that I've been keeping buried deep – an intuition of my wobbling insecurities about letting our son down. About not fucking him up; about making sure he is not like me.

Being in hospital means that I've been opening up to a lot of people recently, telling them my most personal thoughts, letting them see the worst of me. But amidst all of the honesty I've not been able to share this one truth: the extent to which I'm crushed by the responsibility of being a parent; how I'm overwhelmed by the thought of balancing the challenges of parenting with those of running the news desk of a daily newspaper. As we pull out of the hospital grounds, another driver slows her vehicle and waves us onto the road. We slip seamlessly into the line of traffic. I'm going home to see my boy.

***

In the weeks and months after I was released from Ward 12, I had to tell several friends and colleagues where I had been, why I had disappeared from my everyday existence for a week. When I explained that I had been an inpatient in a psychiatric ward, the response was usually one of bemusement, as well sometimes as a reluctance to accept what I was saying. It was as if I was asking them to put together two utterly irreconcilable concepts. I was told more than once that I was the most 'together' person that they had ever met. That I seemed to have the perfect life – a wonderful wife, a beautiful baby boy, a top job, a great house – yet it had all fallen apart. I heard the same response over and over. 'You're the last guy we ever thought this would happen to.' That didn't make me feel much better at the time, but it did start me wondering if there would be some value in me sharing my story with more people.

As it turned out, having to confront the reality of ending up in Ward 12 was the starting point in a process which led to me giving up a successful media career to look after my son – and, ultimately, to the writing of this book. When you're sick, it seems natural to make a change. I was forced to recognise that trying to square the corporate lifestyle of an ambitious journalist with my need to be a good father was tearing me to pieces. (That is not to say it can't be done, merely that I was lousy at finding that balance.) I'd tried numerous medications and techniques to combat crippling depression and anxiety – but nothing seemed to work. As I helplessly witnessed the person I believed I was slipping further and further away, I decided, out of desperation, to walk away from my career. To recalibrate my priorities.

So, did it work? Well, one set of worries was replaced by another. How would I pay the mortgage? How would I support my family? On a few occasions I woke up sweating in the dark of night, thinking, 'Good Christ, what have I done?' But slowly, over the months, I did start to feel better on most days. It turned out that there was a life beyond being in an office. Beyond budgets, rotas and deadlines. I was more relaxed, gentler and a better father, I think. The radical shift in the direction of my life didn't heal me, but it did afford me the space to recognise that perhaps I was not a lost cause after all.

With this came two further important realisations. Firstly, that raising my son is the most important thing I will ever do. I have one child (and an abundance of wonder and respect towards those who manage to raise several!). Meeting his needs, nurturing his character and trying to help prepare him to deal with this world is, for me, a better and healthier way to spend my time than in a boardroom.

I thought I had a big job, but I gave it up to concentrate on the top job.

The second insight I had is that the stigma and misunderstanding around mental health only flourishes when people (particularly men) refuse to talk about it. And yet it is only by talking, or in my case, writing about it, that the taboos can be broken down and a better understanding achieved. Some of the incidents I record in these pages, such as my time in Ward 12, will, I imagine, be difficult for many to read – just as they were difficult for me to write about. But relating them, writing them down, has been for me a key part of a necessary process of coming to terms with the fearfulness of my own brain. In seeking recovery, my discovery has been that when the torment is turned into black words on a white page, it loses much of its power and control over me. And my hope too is that writing about my experiences here will help others to find their own unique path to dealing with mental health difficulties.

But this is not a guidebook or a manual. It is not a self-help book about how to heal yourself from depression, or a manifesto for ditching the corporate treadmill in search of a deeper, simpler meaning to life, or a guide to being a perfect parent. It is just my account of a series of things that happened to me. How I suffered a breakdown. How, even as a patient in a psychiatric ward, I overcame the terror of losing my freedom. It's about how I walked away from a career I had spent two decades building and learned to cope with being a stay-at-home parent. How I became the world's least likely blogger and faced down the trolls who nicknamed me 'The Little Snowflake'. And how, for reasons which I still don't properly understand, I ended up being investigated by social services as an unfit father.

Most of all, this is the story of how in the darkest moments I learnt always to find something to laugh about. How I tried to build a new life, and how I realised that, while I am someone who has battled mental illness for years, it does not mean that I am weaker than anyone else.

Two

The Bus

1981

'Where are you from?'

It's a question we all get asked countless times in our lives. In my own case, I've never been sure how to answer it; how to devise a form of words which gives any clue to the location of the remote, rugged piece of farmland in north Antrim where I grew up. I could say I'm from near the Ballinlea Crossroads, but that is a detail so obscure that I'm not sure it even appears on any map. I've not yet met a person, outside those who live there, who has ever heard of it. It's barely a place at all, just a gathering of fields and a few scattered houses. There are small settlements on all sides – Ballycastle, Ballintoy, Armoy, Glenshesk, Mosside, Dervock, Bushside, Stranocum – but I'm not from any of them. Instead, I fall back on the answer my Da always gave when asked where we were from – 'the arsehole of nowhere'.

I grew up in a large, draughty house at the end of a narrow lane surrounded by sloping fields in the arsehole of nowhere. The nearest dwelling to us was my Granny Peggy's farmhouse at the bottom of our lane, where cats, dogs and poultry wandered free. No other children lived within miles. There was my Da, Ma, my older brother, Stephen and myself in the tall red-brick country house with no heating. My parents were unhappily married and fought incessantly and with the bitterness of those who discover that once youth has been wasted with bad decisions, it can never be retrieved. Stephen and I roamed the muddy fields as young children, playing invented games, climbing trees and setting up hideouts in the roofs of crumbling old stone barns.

Violence was ubiquitous in Northern Ireland in the 1970s and as young boys growing up there, our lives were full of it. Stephen and I fought every day and the outcome was always the same, with my older, stronger brother battering me into tears and submission. We were also regularly hit by both parents and our teachers for every offence, both real and imagined. So was just about every other child I met growing up; beatings were as routine then as the visit of the milkman.

Society was full of violence too. I was born in 1974, one of the worst years of The Troubles. Republican and loyalist paramilitary groups eventually declared ceasefires in 1994. So for the first 20 years of my life, I knew nothing other than the incessant, relentless conflict taking place in the little country where I lived. That doesn't mean it directly touched me, but simply that it was impossible to ignore.

It dominated the news which my Da watched every night on our black-and-white portable telly. It was always on the front page of the large broadsheet newspaper which was delivered to our home each day. I was continually conscious that it was going on. Like the air, it was everywhere. For me, there was no time or existence before 'The Troubles'. The whole of my youth (and that of everyone else of my generation) was completely overshadowed by an inexorable series of shootings, bombings and murders. So common was the violence that one murder on the news was barely even noticed. It had to be a mass atrocity before we would even stop playing. That's all the years of schooling, of playtime, of learning, of joy and wonder. Of innocence. One of the saddest things about adolescence in these circumstances is that you only get one go at it.

I came from a Catholic background. Although my family was mostly irreligious and certainly apolitical, the rules of society dictated that my brother and I should go to a Catholic school. And so, in 1979, I started at St Patrick's Boys' Primary in the nearby town of Ballycastle. Because we lived in the remote countryside, this meant a five-mile bus journey every morning and evening just to get to class and home again. Our peculiar geographic quirk meant that the only bus which serviced our road was the No 171 Ulsterbus, which took the older kids from the neighbouring village of Mosside – where the kerbstones were regularly painted red, white and blue – to Ballycastle High School.

The first challenge was simply getting to the bus. Stephen and I had to walk several miles just to reach the bus stop. Down the long lane, which was pocked by deep puddle holes and lined with wild briar bushes and angry thorns reaching across in an unending quest to scrape skin. Then along the narrow Ballinlea Road in the dark during winter, with no footpaths or streetlights, to reach the little shelter at the distant crossroads. The walk had to be undertaken whatever the weather and, if it rained, by the time we reached the bus stop, clouds of steam would be rising from my wet trousers and my socks would be so saturated that they'd slide off my feet and poke out through the holes in my shoes.

There were certain perils for a young child in walking along that country road. Most of the properties we passed were farms where working or guard dogs patrolled. When I was around eight, I was chased and felled when walking alone early one morning by a huge Alsatian, which left two deep bite marks in my calf. The owner appeared and angrily chastised the hound, ordering it to retreat. But he did not approach me and I was left lying ignored at the side of the road, leaking thin lines of blood. After whimpering for some time, I realised there was nothing else to do but to get up and proceed on my way to the bus stop. I never told anyone that I had been attacked by the dog, assuming that I must have been at fault myself in some way.

But the bus journey itself brought a much deeper terror and this was to be my daily routine for several years. The bus was full of black-blazered High School boys, who were mostly Protestant and often of extreme loyalist conviction. My brother and I were two small primary school children with no interest in religion or politics, but wearing a uniform displaying Catholic religious symbols marked us out as targets for relentless sectarian bullying. By the time we got on the crowded bus there were usually no seats left and we had to stand, ushered down the aisle by unsympathetic drivers towards the oldest boys who sat on the back seat. Many days, before boarding, I remember that I was close to being physically sick, such was my fear of getting on that bus.

Tensions were highest during the republican hunger strikes in the Maze prison in 1981. I was six years old and aware of what was going on in only the vaguest sense. Regardless, as soon as my brother and I boarded the bus every day we were immediately met with a song from the back of the bus which referred to Bobby Sands as a 'dirty Fenian fucker'. I had no idea who Bobby Sands was, but still possessed an innate, youthful understanding that the chants were being recited to frighten me and my brother. There was another song, even more sinister. I've never heard it sung in any other place or at any other time, but the words are still branded into my memory.

'Take the Popey, put him on the table and ram the poker up his hole!

'Ram the poker! Ram the poker! Ram the poker up his hole!'

The boys on the back seat wore heavy black boots which they repeatedly thumped off the floor when they chanted this as if they were hypnotised. To this day I have never witnessed or heard anything else so genuinely chilling and filled with menace. I suppose the boys who were doing it were 15 or 16, but to my child's mind they were giants. I still remember a couple of them, exactly how they looked, their sneering faces filled with hatred. Late every afternoon when my brother and I got off the bus at the end of the return route, several of the kids in the back seat would turn and make obscene or threatening gestures out the back window towards us. Sometimes it was the middle finger. Sometimes they ran a digit across their throats. We knew never to react and simply put our heads down.

The boys from the High School would occasionally fight with those from the Catholic convent secondary school in Ballycastle. Sometimes the convent boys would be waiting to ambush those from the High School when they got off the bus in the morning and my brother and I would have to run to avoid getting caught in the middle of the fistfight. On another occasion the bus was travelling past a housing estate near the convent school when a brick was hurled, shattering one of the windows and showering me with glass. One schoolgirl had to be taken to hospital to be treated for an injury to her eye. The bus driver and several of the High School kids disembarked and spent some time roaming the streets of the housing estate searching unsuccessfully for the person who had thrown the brick. When they returned, a number of remarks and poisonous glances made it clear that, because of my uniform, I was being held partly to blame.

On some occasions the abuse became physical. My brother was pushed around and knocked over a few times. One day my little schoolbag was ripped from my grasp and the contents were scattered. In an effort to recover my exercise and prayer books, I got down on my hands and knees like a desperate starving rat while the mocking laughter was all around.

The events of one afternoon in particular have stayed with me more clearly than any other day. I suspect this episode is one of the few things which will stay vivid in my memory even when everything else begins to fade. On that day, one of the more threatening bullies didn't go to his usual spot at the back of the bus, instead taking a seat just behind where I was standing in the aisle. He tortured me for the whole of the journey home. Pushing and shoving, calling me names. I can still hear the malevolent hiss of his voice. 'Wee Fenian! Wee Fenian!' At one point I felt a tugging at my coat but I was too afraid to turn around.

Eventually the bus pulled to a stop at the crossroads. My brother moved up the aisle to disembark. I tried to follow, but I couldn't. At first, I thought someone was holding me back. But then I saw it was something worse. I used to wear an old faded green anorak, with hanging laces. I saw now that I had been tied by the laces to the seat of the bus. I was just six years old.

I wanted to shout to the driver to hold the bus but I

had no voice. I was frozen with shame and the bus was filled with laughter. I tried to work at the knots but it was hopeless, my tiny fingers felt like they belonged to another. It was the first time I ever saw my own hands tremble.

The situation was horrible. But, in the worst moments, there are often people who are willing to help. A couple of the older girls from the High School came to offer assistance. Their elegant fingers worked at the strings to free me. The driver noticed that I hadn't got off at my usual point. He stopped the bus and came back to see what was happening. I still remember that driver, his face and his name. He was a prominent Orangeman in the area. He asked me if I was alright and I mumbled something in response. He asked who had done this to me. I was about to tell him that I didn't know. But I recall looking up at that moment and seeing the face of my tormentor, grinning at me. I think it was only at this point that I became aware that I wasn't crying. I wasn't going to cry. I found a voice, raised a finger and pointed.

'It was him.'

What happened next is quite direct and more suited to the time it occurred than now, almost four decades later. The driver caught the boy by the collar of his black blazer and dragged him from the seat and up the aisle before he sent him reeling down the bus steps with a solid kick in the arse. He was miles from home but had to walk.

The following day after school my brother and I were waiting for the bus home at the usual time. The routine was that the driver would pick up the High School kids first before driving past the gates of our school to collect us. But this day it was different. The driver, the same man who had ejected my bully on the previous day, reversed the order. He drove past our school first and told us to sit in the front seat, where he could watch over us. It was the only time this ever happened. The only time we ever got to sit at the front of the bus.

***

I suppose an obvious conclusion is that I am recounting these experiences from my early childhood as a starting point for some sort of inexpert explanation for all that comes after: the traumatic moment I can identify when the nuts on the wheels first began to loosen just a little. Maybe that is the case; I really don't know. The truth is that the mind can't be cut open and read like the rings of a tree.

What I do know is that nothing that I experienced or saw in my youth would have been regarded, in my mind or by others, as the least bit remarkable in the time or place I came from. Indeed, it is probably fair to assume my upbringing was not any more unstable than that of the majority of children from my generation and a good deal more stable than many. And perhaps that's the point, that our society then was at every level so inured to dysfunction that the traumatic was given no more thought than the buying of a bag of sweets after school in the little local garage which sold two- and four-star petrol. Damaging emotions were pushed down deep inside us all, never to be processed, dealt with or confronted. Certainly never to be spoken of.

It was only when I became a father myself that I truly began to consider the potentially damaging effects of keeping so much trauma contained, of refusing to recognise or confront what had happened. I'd been attempting to cope with severe depression and anxiety for years but had never been able to satisfactorily pinpoint an origin for my problems.

I remember not so long ago chatting to a friend, someone from outside Northern Ireland. I began to tell her about my experiences on the school bus, of the sectarian bullying, the songs and threatening gestures, about being tied to a seat. As I recounted the story it occurred to me that, although I thought often about the incidents, I had never before shared them with another; I had never properly addressed them at all.

As I rambled on, I noticed that my companion had started to cry. I became disconcerted and embarrassed and asked what was wrong. She told me she was crying because of the cruelty of the story and the helplessness of the young child being viciously bullied. Absurdly, I began to comfort her, to tell her that it was fine, that it had all happened a long time ago and had made no difference to me. It was just a story from another era.

Then she looked at me and said: 'But what if something like that happened to your son?'

Now I was rattled and upset. I mumbled something desperate about how I would never allow it, how I would protect him with every part of my strength. About my fears, as a parent, over the debilitating effects of being bullied.

'Yes,' she replied, 'but it happened to you.'

And I almost replied, without thinking: 'Yes, but that's ok, because it was only me.'

But I stopped myself, realising how weak that statement was. My friend was right, it did happen to me. As did many other things which, up to now, I have been too embarrassed to share with other people. Embarrassed by my own weaknesses, inadequacies and fears. Ashamed of my inability to cope with the most routine aspects of life. I don't know how it all fits together in the mysterious mosaic of my brain, how experience transforms into thoughts, emotions or beliefs about life; how to make sense of it all. But sharing seems like a good starting point.

Three

The Doctor

1993

The woman leans in close to me. She smells of soap and cigarettes.

'How's your mummy's feet? Are they any easier?' she whispers.

'Aye, they're a good bit better now, I think.'

'Will you tell her that I was asking for her? And that I'll maybe see her later in the week if she's up and about.'

'Uh-huh.'

There's nothing for a moment. Then the soapy tobacco smell and another whisper.

'And what are you here for?'

I move uncomfortably in the seat.

'Nothing really, just a check-up.'

I can sense she expects more but I don't provide it. Soon she sniffs, moves her head away and looks in the opposite direction and I feel I can breathe again. But I'm disturbed by the tone of the conversation and begin to nibble at the corner of a fingernail. What if she tells my Ma that she saw me here? How can I explain it? I'll have to think of another lie. I'm overwhelmed with the desire to run away but I simultaneously feel that I haven't the strength to get up. There are maybe 15 people in the room and I know they're all staring in my direction, wondering what is wrong with me. I keep my head down, studying the floor, trying to manage the fear.

I think I know or recognise most of the people here. A couple of my Ma's friends from bingo and a few local mothers accompanying sick, whimpering children. There are some older men who I've seen about the town and a large balding guy who works sometimes with my Da. His right arm is encased in a huge grubby white cast, the result of an incident a few weeks ago when he had an argument with his wife in a pub and then put his fist through the window in the toilet door. When he was thrown out of the bar, he started to hit a brick wall with the same fist until the police came and took him to the hospital. The row was the talk of the town for a while. But here, in this room in which the air seems stale, nobody is talking about it. There's not much talk at all.

The clock high on the far wall tells me that it's more than half an hour after the time I was given for my appointment. I'm both weary over the delay and terrified of it ending. Terrified of the moment when my name is called and I have to explain why I am here.

This is because I am about to do something without precedent in my life. Something which goes against every habit and instinct I possess. I am going, if my courage holds, to tell a doctor how I am feeling. Of course, I've been to the doctor before, I've had the measles, mumps and scarlet fever, but this is different. I'm going to try and explain to him how I'm feeling inside my head. How, at the age of 18, I'm infected by thoughts I can't shift, thoughts which tell me that life isn't worth living anymore. I can't really say when it began. The feelings of worthlessness, of hopelessness and fear seem to have always been there, as much a part of me as the freckles on my arm. A persistent sense of desolation that I've become used to pushing deep down inside, something never to be spoken about or even acknowledged. Not to family or friends, not even to myself. These feelings have always been with me – but there has been something different about this summer. The familiar weight of sadness has been overtaken by thoughts of something much more sinister – the active contemplation of how I will end my own life. There's a local beauty spot on Ireland's north coast – Fair Head, a rugged 200-foot-high sheer cliff where you're more likely to meet a goat than another human. During the sleepless nights and the long, empty days, it is always on this cliff that the scenario is played out over and over in my mind, becoming more and more vivid until it seems inescapable.

Of course, to transfer such thoughts into actions requires some level of motivation, focus and dynamic – attributes which I do not seem to possess. Instead, the summer days have passed with me lying on the sofa in a stupor, disturbed by the thoughts constantly going around my head, but frozen into a state which prevents me being able to do anything which might change or improve my situation. The depression is like a fine layer of dust which covers everything in my life, meaning that the sun doesn't shine brightly, colours are faded, and other people's expressions appear hazy, their words muffled. Everything is dulled and deadened in my world.

I've searched hard for a distraction. The cricket has been on BBC Two this summer. England v Australia: The Ashes. It's an alien sport in the culture in which I've grown up, an impenetrable mystery to every person I know. Yet I've become obsessed by it. From my spot, sprawled on the sofa, I've watched every ball, fixated on how Shane Warne's mastery of leg-spin has tortured the English batsmen; how the home bowling attack has been dismantled by the Aussie top order. I know all the batting averages and the strike rates of the bowlers, and how many catches have been dropped. During the rain interruptions I watch the replays of old test matches, like Botham's Ashes from 1981. The routine of the game and being able to lose myself in the endless statistics have given me some small comfort, but this only serves to make the days when there is no cricket more unbearable. I watch the test matches for hour after hour without emotion or enjoyment, digesting all the data like a computer. It's just something to do.

By this time, my family are living in Ballycastle, a small town clinging to Ireland's north coast. We sold our larger house in the country a couple of years back. One of the reasons for the move was that since my older brother Stephen and I became teenagers, we supposedly needed to be in an environment where there are other young people, not marooned in the lonely countryside. But the move closer to civilisation has only succeeded in pushing me further away from it. Having other children nearby merely emphasises the fact that I have no friends, and some kind of internal block which prevents me from being able to make them easily. My older brother, previously my only companion, now moves in circles of friends which do not include me. These days he usually leaves the house to go 'down the town' in the early afternoon and doesn't return until the small hours of the morning with the smell of drink on his breath. And even when he is home there is little communication between us anymore, just an unspoken awkwardness and embarrassment over previous shared experience. A sense that we know too much about each other's pasts. One day a few months ago, when I was moving his coat off my bed a small object fell from the pocket. I lifted it from the carpet, only to drop it again in shock when I realised it was a condom. I stared at the foil packet, the first time I had ever seen one. It seemed to represent how far apart our different paths had taken us.

***

My name has been called. I slowly walk the few steps towards the surgery before some inbuilt sense of deference makes me knock lightly on the door. There is an edge of harshness in the voice from the other side of the wood. 'Come in, come in!' I enter the brightly lit room. The doctor is at a wooden desk, head down, writing swiftly. He uses a proper fountain pen. I stand uselessly until he looks up and beckons me towards a chair with the wave of a hand. Now he stares at me with dark, severe eyes. His eyebrows lift slightly. Is it surprise or contempt?

'How can I help you today?'

This is the moment which I have been moving towards for most of my life. The moment when I finally take my problems outside of my own head. When I ask for help, find out if a better way exists. But now that it has arrived, all I can focus on is how dry my mouth feels. How the air in this small room seems to be desperately thin, like the top of a mountain, so I can't get a proper breath. I think about my breathing and the eyes of the doctor which are fixed upon me. Each second becomes like a lifetime and I fear that I will be unable to summon any words.

'Well?' the doctor continues.

I stare back at him, my face burning with shame. I hear words being delivered slowly.

'Well. . . I've been feeling a bit down lately. . . I just . . . well, I just get really down.'

'"Down"?' he replies quickly. 'What do you mean, "down"?'

I begin to fall apart under the heat of his dry interrogation. I mumble some more sentences but I know that my complaints are absurd and weak. My speech begins to slow, like a toy when the batteries start to fail. I try to tell him about the dark thoughts of suicide, the crippling lethargy, but he continues to stare without comprehension as my efforts at coherence falter. Soon I give up and let the silence hang between us, waiting for him to bring the torture to an end. He sits back in his chair and looks away, making me think that he feels I'm not worthy of his gaze anymore.

'Have you spoken to your family about this?'

I shake my head. He scans the room again, as if searching for an idea. Then he turns back towards me and sits upright.

'You went to the grammar school, is that right?'

I nod.

'And your predicted exam results are good enough, aren't they?'

I'm not sure if I react to this at all, but he goes on.

'So, in a couple of months you'll be able to go off to university and then after that you can get a job as a teacher and you'll have nothing to worry about.'

Perhaps he sees something in my face, maybe uncertainty or doubt, because his voice hardens slightly as he gestures towards the door.

'You see all the people in that waiting room? How many of them do you think have had the chances that you have? How many of them do you think have had the chance to go to university? Some of them are really sick and they are not talking like this, talking about being "down". When they have a bad day, they just have to get on with it because there's nothing else for it.'

And I know that he is right. At this moment, his logic is undeniable. I have committed one of the deadliest sins by trying to talk about it, by not being stoic, by displaying weakness in front of another. My problems are mine alone, they are not to be shared. There is to be no empathy, no support in this struggle. All my life, in my mind, I've been digging holes to hide my defects from the rest of the world. Now I know the next hole I dig will be the deepest yet.

I mumble some form of goodbye and reach for the door handle. I have been in the room for less than five minutes, perhaps less than three. Curious faces rise to meet me in the waiting room as I stumble out. I'm convinced every person has heard every word and I am sure there are sniggers. I rush out of the building with my head down, afraid that I'm about to cry in front of others, gasping for the clean air outside. I've just reached the carpark when I hear a familiar voice.

'Well, did you get sorted ok? The doctors are all so lovely here, aren't they? Here, will you tell your mummy this for me. . .'

It's soapy tobacco woman. She has come outside for a cigarette and is moving towards me, a terrible smile on her face. She wants to talk. So much shared information, but so little understanding of anything of worth. I begin to run, trying to get away from her as fast as I can. I'm done with talking, there is no value in it.

It will be more than two decades before I again dare to tell another human being what is going on inside my head.

Four

At Work

March 2013

I'm in a large room with a large table. Several serious-faced people are sitting around it, frowning as they study sheets of paper filled with long lines of numbers. There's a woman talking: a calm, steady monotone, without variation.

'Now look at the spreadsheet on the second page, go to the second column across and the fifth figure down. . .'

I glance at the person beside me, to make sure I'm on the right page. I'm not. I shuffle through the sheets and pretend that I'm following the presentation, nodding along at what I imagine are the right times. All I can see are endless long, meaningless numbers which I have no ability to process into a useful form. All industries, even those that are built around words, are defined by the numbers. And I have no gift with numbers, no ability to line them up and order them, to make them do what I want. I just stare at the page, utterly lost.

There's some more discussion and then a man at the head of the table talks with authority.

'Well, that's where we are this month. Anybody got any thoughts? What about Editorial? Jonny?'

Hearing my name stirs me from my confused stupor, like the naughty schoolboy at the back of the class who has been singled out by the teacher. I sit upright and flick through some pages in front of me nervously.

'Well,' I begin hesitantly, 'it's good . . . but I think we can always do better.'

There's a murmur of agreement around the table which encourages me. I feel a little pulse of rebellion so I decide to continue.

'The main thing is it's washing its own face, but if we peel the onion we should be able to get a helicopter view of the issues. Some blue sky thinking by the top team and we ought be able to drill down into it and come up with an action plan to target the low-hanging fruit. Some joined up thinking is what we need.'

There's the same murmur of appreciation and nodding of heads.

'Thanks, Jonny,' the man at the top of the table says. 'We'll certainly action that.'

I can't do numbers but I've always been able to do things with words. That's why I became a newspaper journalist. That's what enabled the meek teenager who spent so much time obsessing over how he would kill himself, who fell apart in the doctor's surgery twenty years earlier, to build a successful media career.

***

Months after I visited that doctor during that long-distant summer, I moved to Belfast to study history and politics at Queen's University – the first person from my family to experience life as a student. Three years passed in a blur of alcohol, misery and discovery. Perhaps I had never expected to get that far because it was only after I graduated that I was forced to confront the reality that I had no idea what to do with the rest of my life. I promptly signed on the dole.

My continuing lack of focus led to some unfulfilling early employment experiences. I worked as a van driver delivering supplies to Chinese restaurants, a job which led to me damaging my back carrying large drums of vegetable oil, boxes of frozen chips and bags of bean sprouts. Then I was a labourer on a building site, a shop assistant in a video store and a caller in a bingo hall, before deciding I needed a structured career path. I trained in print journalism and secured a job in a small weekly newspaper. Within a couple of years, I had moved on to a daily newspaper and was rising quickly through the ranks. First a reporter, then a security correspondent, then a news editor. By my mid-30s I was Deputy Editor of the biggest newspaper in Northern Ireland.

Colleagues assumed I was ambitious and assured. It may have come across that way but the truth was very different. I never had any confidence in my own ability. Every day of my career was the day I believed I would be discovered; the day when my incompetence and idiocy would finally be revealed to all. But there was also a comfort in the monotonous routine of office employment. By throwing myself into my work, I was able to cover up many of the insecurities which had plagued my earlier life. I had found something to which I belonged, and I clung to it like a drowning man to a piece of driftwood. Some of my obsessive personality traits began to take hold. I worked long hours. In truth, I did very little else. It was at the office that I was lucky enough to meet Debs. We fell in love and got married. The fact that she worked in the same industry, and seemed to understand my obsession with work, made the transition to married life easier.

During these years, the most terrifying parts of my own mind were still there, but I mostly ignored them. I still endured the darkness, the times when I was certain I could not go on. The daily thoughts of suicide never left me but I learnt to bypass them because I was doing something useful. The dark thoughts blended into my routine, but were always there, ongoing, automatic, like breathing, known only to myself. Everyone else saw me as strong, the steady one. But I was ill-fitted to that role. Patching over a pothole is only ever a temporary solution. Sooner or later the cracks will reopen, wider than before.

**

Back to the meeting that day, and I'm studying numbers on a spreadsheet. But I can't bury the insistent thought that it's the newsroom where I really need to be, because I've got nothing for tomorrow's front page. The next item on the agenda for the 'Boardroom Executive Meeting' is a presentation about new digital technology which should help our business. The lights are switched off and a laptop beams a video tutorial onto a white screen. I try to force myself to concentrate but within seconds I'm hopelessly lost again.

As I have climbed higher in my chosen profession, the pressure and responsibility has grown, as has the number of people who depend on me. By this time, I've come to believe that the whole process of the paper coming out, day after relentless day, depends on me being there at all times, always giving more and more of myself. But I've recently noticed my behaviour becoming erratic, my power to think logically starting to break down. On some days I feel that I am close to spent, mentally exhausted, but I see no alternative other than to keep going, harder than ever. The bucket has been filled too high, and now the dirty, black water is starting to spill out, to cascade around me dangerously.

I can't remember the last time I slept. I don't recall the last time I ate a meal. Having never smoked in my life, in the past few months I've developed a 40-a-day habit. I've never been much of a drinker but I now consume a couple of bottles of red wine most evenings. I've started going for long walks late at night, with no destination in mind and no expectation that I will return home. Often, I almost don't. Other evenings I just sit in my back garden into the small hours, drinking and smoking. On many nights, I burst into tears and sob for what seems like hours.

But still, I keep my behaviour and thoughts from everyone. My wife, my family, my colleagues. The pressure is intense but I still keep turning up for work on time. Making decisions, leading a team, being the responsible, dependable one. And, even as my mental state has started to collapse, I've been called upon to take on more and more responsibilities – meetings in the boardroom, attending conferences, making broadcast appearances, managing budgets, taking big decisions. I'm always the first one in the office each morning. As my colleagues arrive, they pass me and say hello, or ask how I'm doing. I always smile and answer the same way ... 'I'm fine.'

***

Now a chirpy female voice is talking over the moving images. I keep hearing the word 'algorithm', again and again. Soon I give up any chance of understanding and fish my phone from a jacket pocket. I've been in this room for more than 90 minutes now and I'm due in the Editor's office for news conference in another half-hour. That is when tomorrow's front page will be decided on. I'm feeling increasingly anxious because I know I've got nothing good – no big story, no idea, not even a lead to follow. I need to be in the newsroom finding content, instead I'm marooned in the boardroom listening to someone talking about algorithms.

I see that there are several messages and missed calls on my phone – journalists looking for instructions, contacts with information or tips. Under the boardroom table I start pounding out a series of texts: *Stuck in a meeting. I'll be out soon. Call you in ten.* There's also a message from Debs, my heavily pregnant wife who is at home, due to give birth in just a few weeks' time: *Hi honey, how are you? What time will you be home? Xxx.* I type and send a quick response without looking at the screen. I can feel my anxiety levels beginning to spike alarmingly, as I try to work out how much time I've got left in the day and how much I've still got to do. But these numbers, like those on the spreadsheet, just don't add up for me.

My bowels are churning and for one terrible moment I fear I might shite myself right here in the boardroom, in front of all the commercial people. There's a particular oppression about this kind of work – it's the desperate pressure of knowing that I need to find an idea. The relentless burden of always having to produce, the ever-present fear that this is the day I just won't be able to do it anymore.

Working in newspapers is like being stuck in a Sisyphean loop – every day you push the boulder of inspiration up the hill, but it rolls back down each time, so the next morning you have to start from the beginning again. And it never ends. There's a dream I've been having for years. A dream where I'm about to present my ideas to a room full of stern and unforgiving bosses, and I've got nothing, other than a blank sheet of paper. Every time I try to type something on the sheet the words just melt away. I usually wake up at the point where I'm walking into the room to meet my interrogators with the blank sheet of paper. I'm never able to get back to sleep afterwards.

***

Eventually the presentation ends and the boardroom meeting breaks up. Some of the other people in the room hang around, chatting, nibbling on biscuits and sipping tea. But I dash away without a word and rush up the stairs, pushing through the heavy double doors into the newsroom. Here the lethargy is so thick I can almost smell it, a collective sense of relaxation has taken hold due to the boss – me – having been away. Before I've even reached my seat, the newsroom secretary has intercepted me and is thrusting several small pieces of paper into my hand. A series of messages and notes; people wanting to speak to the person in charge. She points to one message at the top of the pile.

'Can you phone this woman? She's been on several times . . . We did a story about her son's death and she's very upset. I think you should call her.'

'OK, just give me a few minutes and I'll do it.'

There's now less than 20 minutes until the news conference. I bring my news list up on the computer screen, reminding myself of what I haven't got. I quickly scan the emails and the wire services and check the news websites, but there's just not much happening. People often ask me how I cope on really busy news days, the occasions when there's a big story. But that's easy, it's just a matter of writing about it. It's the quiet news day which is a journalist's worst nightmare. The paper still has to come out.

I go for a walk around the room, speaking to reporters and trying to rouse some creative thinking from the staff. But they're passive today, waiting to be told what to do rather than driving the news agenda. I know that the idea is going to have to come from me. I get on my mobile and make a few quick calls to various contacts. I pick up a few snippets, interesting pieces of gossip and possible leads to follow. But I need something strong which can be put together quickly, not an investigative tip which is going to take weeks of work.

I go back to my desk where the same secretary is still waiting for me, waving the piece of paper with the woman's phone number and fixing me with a disapproving look. There's so little time and my nerves are ragged but I know I've got no choice but to make the call; it's the honouring of the link a media organisation has with its audience. I dial the number and introduce myself to the woman on the other end of the line. I can tell from her voice that she has been crying.

'Are you the person in charge?' she asks, her voice breaking.

It's not the moment to explain the multi-layered intricacies of the management structure of a media organisation, so I just tell her that yes, I am. She struggles to recount to me the facts about the death of her young son in an accident, about the terrible impact it had on her family. Then she tells me about her disgust at seeing a story about it in our newspaper, and how this made everything worse for her family.

'It was like twisting the knife even deeper,' she tells me.

I've dealt with many calls like this before, probably dozens. As always, I now take the time to explain the guidelines for reporting deaths, how the feelings of the grieving family are balanced against the public's right to information. About how we strive to be as sensitive as possible in our reporting; about how the same methodology is used by every single other newspaper. But the truth is, my words sound mechanical and weak, like I'm reading from a tired script. I'm not the person to do this job. How can I relate to or empathise with a grieving mother, when my ability to deal with other people on an emotional level has all but collapsed?

The woman listens with obvious contempt before she snaps at me again. 'You're just a slippery salesman. All you're trying to do is sell papers.'

Which is undeniably true. We're a daily newspaper trying to survive in a crowded market, just like the others. All of the numbers on those spreadsheets – this is what they amount to in my world. It is ingrained in journalists to peddle in grief, in human suffering, and to repackage it for mass consumption. As I listen to this grieving mother I think about my wife and unborn child and I experience a deep sense of shame and self-loathing. If the only defence we have is, 'Well, this is what we do', then there's no defence at all.

I let the woman throw insults at me for a few more minutes. I listen to every word and I'm unfailingly polite and desperately trying to be sympathetic – but there's now less than ten minutes until news conference and I've still got nothing. But I make a point of giving her the contact details of the regulatory body which she can contact if she believes our coverage has been unfair. I'm not sure she's listening. And even this is a snake-oil trick because I'm confident we've broken none of the rules of the code of conduct and, even if we had, the process of lodging a complaint is so laborious and the possible penalties so mild as to make it almost pointless. In truth it's just a tactic to get her off the phone.

She senses I'm trying to bring the call to an end and resists, demanding some sort of resolution or redress. But eventually she runs out of steam. 'You know, you're nothing but a cowardly bastard,' she hisses before hanging up.

I replace the receiver and notice the secretary is already moving towards me with more scraps of paper, but I wave her away with a weary hand. I'm just not able to deal with any more of it today. As I said, I've taken dozens of calls like this but I never get used to them, never develop a thick enough skin to protect me from the inevitable anger of the unfortunate families who have their business pored over on our pages by countless readers. The sound of this upset mother's voice, the phrase 'cowardly bastard', keep going around and around in my mind.

There's little more than five minutes until conference and I've still got nothing. I know that I haven't got the time but I decide I need to be alone and I desperately want a smoke, so I leave the newsroom and head for the roof. I emerge onto the smoking area, a little covered spot on the top of the building with ashtrays and chairs. I light a cigarette and walk to the far corner of the roof where I can get a proper view of the Belfast landscape. I see the new buildings mixed with the old ones to the north, an army of cranes stretching towards the sky, transforming the city where I have spent my adult life.

I climb onto a smaller, raised concrete area which brings me to the edge of the roof and I lean against a little wall which allows me to see onto the ground below. The familiar thought passes through my mind – about how simple it would be to make all the pain and the anxiety go away. I close my eyes and the mild spring breeze is welcome against my face.

I step back from the edge and take long draws from my cigarette. My mind is raw, but utterly alert now. I force myself to concentrate. All of the other shit melts away, I just need to think about a line for the front page; nothing else matters. I consider what's in the news, what's on my list, what I've got to work with. I take a final suck on the cigarette and flick the end towards an ashtray before I start to walk back into the building. It's time for conference and I think I've got the beginnings of an idea.

Five

The Birth

May 2013

A gentle touch on the shoulder wakes me in the night. I'm momentarily confused, perhaps a little afraid, disorientated by the depth of the darkness. My wife whispers just two words.

'It's started.'

Without the need for further explanation, I go and run the bath, steam urgently rising, a thick film coating the mirror like sauce on a spoon. I help Debs into the tub and squeeze her hand as she bravely grimaces through the discomfort of the early contractions. We smile at each other nervously. We are ready to meet our firstborn child, to find out if we will have a son or a daughter.

I could say it's about time. It's already two weeks past the due date. Our old life is stubbornly clinging on before it's banished forever. Never have days moved so slowly. Perhaps it's just a little preview of the way things are going to be from now on. Our new son or daughter keeping us ever alert, teasing and torturing us until our nerves are stretched taut only to collapse into a loose and flabby pulp.

***

Two hours later, the spring sun is inching above the tops of houses and we've arrived at the hospital maternity unit. We're shown to a small grey room and told to sit and wait.

So we wait. A friendly woman in a blue uniform offers us tea and toast. Debs accepts but I shake my head, my stomach too twisted to consider food. I have to force down some spasms of nausea at the sight and smell of the flecks of pale butter melting into the crimson jam. I try to distract myself by reading the posters on the wall. 'Breast feeding is best'; 'Planning a water birth?' I check my phone. There are several messages from work. I read the first. *We're snowed under today. Are you able to come in?* I put the phone back in my pocket.

Later in the morning we're taken to a bed on a busy ward. Beside us, on the other side of a thin, shabby curtain, I hear a woman softly crying. A midwife comes to examine my wife. I attempt to start a conversation with her, to get some information about the process, but she's clearly harried and the answers are short. She tells us we could have quite a long wait before it's time. Our early excitement is now slightly blunted.

We talk to each other. The same conversations about the future we've been having for months, just a little more subdued. Then Debs falls into a light and fitful sleep. I look around. Up to this moment I've been in a hospital ward perhaps less than ten times in my life. Visiting sick relatives, always desperate for the encounter to end, scurrying away as quickly as it was decent to do so.

l gaze out of the window. The day is sunny now. A fine spring morning quickly ripening in the glare. The breeze is nothing more than a whisper among the leaves. The sort of day which seems filled with unexplained promise, which makes you feel that you can be a better person. But my nerves are too ragged to enjoy the warm air. The staff move around me stoically, trying to deal with problems which are arising more quickly than they can be solved.

Sporadically I hear the confused and anguished wails of a newborn child and the quieter sobs of relieved, joyful parents.

We stumble on through the hours, into the afternoon and then evening. Debs slips in and out of sleep, occasionally holding an oxygen mask to her face to relieve the discomfort of the contractions. I feel useless and foolish as I sit there stroking her hand. I watch midwives start and finish their shifts. I watch the sun rise through the windows at one side of the building and later see it sink through the windows at the other. My wife is becoming more and more uncomfortable and afraid. I suppose I'm too timid and polite to raise much fuss, to add to the obvious burden. After several hours without contact, an older midwife approaches us and speaks with calm authority. She is reassuring and lovely and tells us that our child will be born on this day. On the Friday. We feel better. Then she leaves and we never see her again.

The sun has disappeared completely. Much later, deep into the evening, Debs is examined by a doctor – the first to approach us since our arrival. His face betrays a degree of concern, but I can't tell if this is specific to us or the general state of affairs around him on the ward. I ask him if there is anything to be concerned about and he responds with the shortest shake of his head, barely noticeable. He says he wants to monitor the baby's heartbeat and attaches a machine to Debs. He tells her that she is making progress and just has to be patient.

So I sit there beside my wife for more hours, watching needles on the machine scratch-coloured lines onto a long roll of white paper. Sometimes the lines are close together, plodding along slowly like a lazy stream, on other occasions the needles twitch agitatedly and the lines veer wildly apart, causing me alarm. I look around but nobody ever comes to check the lines.

Close to midnight a nurse asks me to leave the ward. Fathers are not allowed to stay overnight. Debs, already distressed and exhausted, is now close to hysterical, terrified at the thought of being made to face the most vulnerable hours alone. And I am very reluctant to go; it seems inhumane to separate us now. Eventually, after Debs is given an injection to help her sleep, I agree to leave rather than cause a disturbance for other patients.

I spend the night shifting uneasily in my car in the hospital car park, separated from my scared and lonely wife by concrete and glass. On the Saturday morning before the birds have found their voice, I'm standing haggard and unshaven outside the doors of the ward again. Soon I'm right back at the bedside offering my useless platitudes. There are only so many times you can tell someone, 'It's going to be alright', before they can reasonably tell you to, 'Shut the fuck up!'.

It's mid-morning before Debs is eventually moved to her own room. Finally, something seems to be happening, more than 30 hours after the labour began. There's a little radio beside the window and I tune it to Radio Two and Graham Norton. His pleasant southern Irish lilt seems to relax Debs more effectively than I can – and I'll always be grateful to him for that. Things feel a little brighter now. I walk up and down the ward corridor. It's sunny again today.

A nurse tells me to take a break. It hasn't occurred to me until this moment that it's been more than a full day since I've eaten. I walk to the hospital canteen and nibble on the corner of a triangle of burnt toast. A bitter black coffee restores something within me and I watch a group of nurses at a nearby table having their tea break, chatting and laughing with each other, with the kind of intimacy that only shared experience can bring. As I walk back towards the little room, I can feel the excitement beginning to rise in me again – but this is quickly shattered when I'm intercepted near the door by a nurse with a serious expression who tells me not to panic.

I enter the room where Debs is crying. Apparently, the baby has been showing signs of distress and a young female doctor from Bangladesh is extracting blood from the child's head inside my wife's body. For a moment, things seem to calm down before the commotion begins again and the process is repeated, with nurses walking urgently in and out of the room.

The need for an epidural is raised. It is not part of our plan but Debs is now so enervated and riven with pain that she agrees without hesitation. An anaesthetist arrives and begins the process of freezing her spine. Her pain is soon relieved but the alarm over the baby has not diminished. As they go on with the process of sticking a large needle into our unborn child's head, something in me finally fractures. I ask the doctor if it would not be better for everyone if they would just deliver the baby now. She simply smiles and assures me that we were not at that stage yet.

The process stutters on for another hour – periods of quiet, interrupted by short moments of hurried animation when the baby's distress levels increase. Finally, at some point in the afternoon, the doctor stands up and says that we have to get into theatre for a Caesarean section; that the health of the child depends on getting him or her delivered as soon as possible. My wife has been in labour for more than 35 hours. I'm aware that people are now moving swiftly around me. I stand there, confused, as a blue gown and mask are thrust into my hands. Eventually a sympathetic nurse dresses me and rushes me into a brightly lit operating room.

I stand on one side of a blue screen beside a bed, talking gently to Debs. I'm aware of movement, some conversation and then a pathetic little cry of protest. A doctor is holding something up, a tiny purple ball of rage which resembles nothing. I force myself to refocus on the object. Then I see a scrotum.

'It's a boy!' I try to shout but my voice is trembling. 'It's a boy!'

He's covered in shit so has to be cleaned up and weighed before he's wrapped in a blanket and given to me. I brace myself for a weight but he's as light as foam. One of his little eyes is swollen shut and there are angry red scrapes across his scalp from where the blood was removed with the needle, reminding me that it hasn't just been Debs who has been put through agony. He peers angrily at me through his one open eye, as if everything in the world is my fault. It's a look I will become accustomed to over the years. I whisper into his tiny soft ear. 'Hello, son, I'm your daddy.' It's the best I can come up with. Then I place him on his mummy's chest, his little angry red face sinking into the familiar warmth. They deserve to be together.

The doctors and midwives congratulate me and then get ready to move on to the next family. It's been the most emotional experience of my life, but it's just a job for them, something which happens in this building dozens of times every day. I struggle to accept that anyone else has ever been through this experience before, that this feeling is not entirely individual to me. Soon we're moved back to the ward and people start arriving with balloons and teddies. But we don't really want to see anyone; we just want to rest and be together. Like a family.

For the first few hours our son James doesn't make a sound. He just watches everything, taking it all in. Very late that night I eventually get home, just to grab a few hours of sleep. Debs and James are being kept in hospital. I'm worn out but sustained by delirium. I can't wait to get back to the ward and I arrive early the next morning laden down with new supplies and presents.

But I hear the noise before I'm even close to the bedside.

He has started crying. The kind of crying that, once it begins, you fear will never stop.

Six

The Hot Night

July 2013

It's been the best spell of weather we've had in years. Just like the hot summers I remember from when I was a child. In recent years, my Da has taken to saying there aren't really proper seasons anymore. They're all the same, without definition, he insists. It's all cold, grey summers and mild winters now, and endless days of fine drizzle which never seems to go away. But this is a proper summer, with sunshine so strong it makes the tar on the roads melt and opens cracks on the lawn so wide you can fit your hand into them.

At work we've been running stories about the weather every day, finding ever more exotic locations which are colder than it is in Northern Ireland. 'What a scorcher! Today we're hotter than Ibiza'; 'No end to heatwave in sight: Belfast hotter than Cairo!' Everyone is talking about the weather, so it seems the natural thing to write about. But after four or five days the ideas aren't rolling from my mind so readily. 'Fears over hosepipe ban'; 'Sales of ice-cream soar'; 'Ten ways to stay cool in the office' . . .

It is early evening and I am leaving the office, hours after I've promised my wife I'd be home. The muggy blast hits me as soon as I push my way through the revolving door, like the feeling you get when you step off the airplane on a foreign holiday. Like walking into a wall of hot air. I remove my tie. Debs is using the family car, so I have the convertible today. I hit the button and the roof slides away quietly. As I start the engine, I exchange a few words with the security guard. He is also keen to talk about the weather.

'It's too hot; we're not built for this weather.'

Not wanting to seem contrary, I simply nod. I'm almost out of the carpark when my phone rings for the first time this evening. I answer without needing to look at the caller ID. It's one of the guys at work, wanting to check a detail in tomorrow's paper. I'm friendly, calm and deliberate, going through the instructions, just as I did before I left ten minutes ago. I know this will be the first of several such calls tonight. They all know what to do but there's always an inherent reluctance to be the person making the decision.

The phone rings again when I'm on the motorway, and once again, as I'm pulling the car into the driveway of our house. I sit there in the vehicle for a couple more minutes, discussing a late-breaking story and what we need to shift around to make space for it. I'm assessing its import, its worth. Is it better than what we've got? There's a silence on the other end of the line as they wait for me to make a call on it. Then I'm through the front door and there's Debs, walking up and down the hallway, gently rocking two-month-old James on her shoulder, encouraging him towards sleep. She looks exhausted, ragged with the demands of giving constant attention to another.

I apologise for being so late before I take over, softly singing to James as Debs gets herself something to eat. I've got no appetite myself.

We briefly share details of the day, before she goes for a lie-down. The arrangement is that I sit up to give James his late evening feed, then Debs feeds him in the middle of the night, and then I'm there to do the early morning bottle before I go to the office. I set him in the little basket but he begins to cry immediately, his features snarling. He prefers to be carried. I lift him again and walk from room to room, humming a little tune while his toothless gums gnaw at my finger. It might be 'The Grand Old Duke of York' or 'Baa Baa Black Sheep' – I'm not sure.

I feel my phone buzzing in the breast pocket of my shirt, so I shift James to my right arm and hold it against my left ear. It's the office again. The breaking story is developing – might it be something for the front page? I can't seem to clear my mind, so I tell them that I'll think about it and call back.

James is crying more persistently now, so I decide to feed him. I go to get a bottle from the fridge, the cool air surprising me when I open the door. The fridge bulb is broken, so I have to turn on the main kitchen light. The bottle I prepared this morning is lying on its side and the milk has leaked out, all over the butter and the yoghurt and onto the chicken. I lift the bottle and notice that I hadn't attached the blue lid properly. My son is bawling against my ear and the sound seeps through my skull, sticking to my brain like mould on a damp wall.

'Ah, for fuck's sake,' I whisper to myself, leaning my head against the door of the fridge, fighting back the familiar despair. I go to the front room and set James in his basket, placing a little teddy by his arm. The protest begins immediately but I have to leave him. I remove and wipe all the food from the fridge, throwing out a couple of items which are saturated with baby formula. Then I take out the glass shelves and wash them in soapy water in the metal sink under the tap. Then I scoop yellow-white powder into a new, sterilised bottle, counting out the capfuls under my breath. I boil the kettle and mix the formula. James is screaming from the other room, but the bottle is much too hot. I talk to him as I run it under the cold-water tap.

'I'm coming, wee man, I'm going as fast as I can. Daddy's coming.'

The bottle seems to take forever to cool. I'm talking to my son and sprinkling drops of milk onto my wrist in growing agitation. When I finally go to lift him, he is kicking his puny little legs angrily in the air, fuming at the neglect. I remove my shirt before I gather him in my arms, giving comfort to him with the warmth of my skin.

It's only now I notice that the heavy sun is sinking towards the horizon and the last of the evening haze is disappearing. We sit in the half-light, his little body wriggling against mine as he sucks impatiently at the bottle. I feed him just a little before I place him on my shoulder, rubbing his weak back, feeling his cheek burning at my neck. He lies there, as if he's part of my body, until I hear a short burp escape. Then we repeat the process again and again, until I sense the urgent sucking at the bottle beginning to slow and I know he's satisfied. I change his nappy and outfit before I carry him and the basket upstairs. I place it on a metal stand beside Debs, who is sleeping on top of the covers. I walk around the room with my son in my arms, until I feel the fight go out of him and his arms become limp. Then I lay him down, gently kissing each cheek and his forehead.

'Night, night, son, Daddy loves you very much.'

I say a few words to Debs and she mumbles a response, but I don't think she really knows I'm there. Then I go down the stairs again, put my shirt back on and leave the house. It's late but the temperature has barely dropped. I can feel a line of perspiration forming along my spine. Within minutes the shirt is damp and clinging to my skin. I walk. Like I do most nights. Towards the end of our estate and slowly up the hill towards the dual carriageway. The briars at the ditches have not been cut and their thorny arms are reaching across the pavement, so I have to step onto the road to avoid them. I'm not going anywhere in particular. I've got no distance or route in mind. It's more a form of escape, like a trick I try to play on my own mind. Pretending for a while that I can simply walk away from it all.

I go for a long time without really focusing, lost in my own thoughts, until I notice I'm approaching the motorway. I climb the slip road and begin to cross the bridge above the four lanes. Just over halfway across, I stop and lean on the metal rails, watching the road below. There are few cars at this time of night. The occasional lorry heading towards Dublin, headlights cutting long, thin holes in the gathering dusk.

I stay like this for a long time, looking first into the distance until I see the coming glare of a vehicle and then following it as it approaches and then disappears from my view. I take out my phone to check the time. It's well after 10.00 p.m. and I notice there are half a dozen missed calls. I've forgotten about work. I phone the office and make some decisions, doing it quickly and automatically. I hang up and pocket the phone, taking one more look at the motorway before I start to walk back. There's a hole in one of my shoes and it's making my foot feel sore, but I keep my pace even. I want to get to the shop before it closes and suddenly I'm feeling a burn of panic that I might not make it.

The route seems longer going back but eventually I see the bright sign and the lights. I go into the shop. It's empty, except for the man mopping the floor who seems pained that I've arrived so late. I mumble an apology about stepping across the floor and ask for two packs of cigarettes and two bottles of red wine. I know one of each won't be enough to get me through the night.

Within minutes I'm back home and quickly go up to the bedroom. James and Debs are asleep, both breathing deeply, in time with each other. I kiss my wife on the head and she mumbles something at me before I leave them. I go down to the kitchen and select a glass, rinsing it under the cold tap before I take my shopping into the back yard. The little canvas chair is on the decking, my small, battered radio sits underneath, beside a cracked plate I use as an ashtray.

I adjust the dial on the wireless, needing to find something which is just music. No talking. I settle on an unknown channel, setting the volume so it's only just audible. I begin to smoke and drink, alternating between long drags of the cigarette and gulps of the sickly wine. When I finish one cigarette, I immediately light another, counting the number of the thin white sticks down until I'm into the second box. There's no contentment or comfort in the habit.

***

It's much later now. I've been sitting this way for two or three hours when I hear the beginning of a song on the radio, something I think I might recognise from many years back. I turn up the volume slightly to listen to the slow, melancholic melody. I don't know what the song is supposed to be about, but I find my own connection with it and soon I'm weeping. Just softly and silently at first. A tear inches down my cheek and it's not unpleasant. But soon it gives way to deep sobs – a paroxysm of weeping, afflicting my whole person, making my chest tremble and restricting my breathing. This is the laying bare of the part of me that nobody else ever sees or knows about. The part which exists in eternal terror, which tells me every moment of every day that I can't go on. The part of my being which keeps telling me I'll never be good enough. The part I've always kept secret.

Eventually the tears run dry and my body aches from the effort. I light another cigarette and check my phone. It's the middle of the night. In just a couple of hours, James will be awake and I'll have to go to work shortly after that. I'm exhausted but I know I won't be able to sleep now. So I might as well stay where I am. Sitting here in the dark.

Seven

The Breakdown

September 2013

I'm in the house on my own when the shaking begins. Debs has taken James to her parents because I told her I wanted to be alone. This is how pathetic I am. It is easier to pretend that I don't love my family than it is to tell them that there is something wrong inside my head. Easier to make them go away when I'm having a bad day than to admit my weakness.

I try to fall into my usual ritual of drinking and smoking, just to help me to get through the evening, but I can't settle in my spot in the back yard. My mind is too agitated. I have to stand, to keep moving, walking in circles, mumbling to myself, biting my hand. I only realise I am doing this when blood begins to stream down my thumb and stain my shirt sleeve. But I am inured against any sort of physical pain.

I'm standing in the hallway with a view through the kitchen window of the orange sun setting when the certainty of imminent death presents itself in my mind. It's not like I've made a decision or even had a conscious thought about it. It's just there, as inevitable and natural as the descent of the sun on the other side of the glass.

I've dealt with thoughts of my own death for most of my life – I've even been close to realising them a few times. But I feel that this, now, is different. It is incontrovertible and suffocating. I can see nothing else now, no other way.

I rest my head against the wall. Then I slide to the floor so my face is against the tiles. I close my eyes and think about how I will end my life tonight. I'm so tired of it all.

And that's when the shaking starts. At first, I don't think this is anything unusual – I often get trembling hands when my mind is under duress. I've had embarrassing encounters before when I've had to hide my hands under my desk at work or have been left unable to use cutlery in a restaurant. It's a familiar part of any panic attack.

But this trembling soon deteriorates into something much worse: a violent, jerking motion which makes my shoulders ache. It's more like a convulsion, a seizure, a possession. I lie there on the floor, eyes open now, watching the actions of my own hands with terrible fascination.

Then I have a thought; a question for myself. Is this something that is happening to me – or something that I am making happen? Are my hands out of my control or have I made a decision that they should shake? I'm suddenly fascinated by the distinction and I start to tell myself that I can stop my hands shaking at any moment. I can do it if I want to. I keep having this thought, yet my hands keep shaking. I'm sure I can stop it. But I can't.

My thought process deepens. Now I'm wondering is this my version of a cry for help, a physical manifestation of something that my brain cannot comprehend confronting. A signal to others. Is this an act of defiance? A refusal to give in?

I scramble onto my side. I know my phone is in the back pocket of my jeans but the task of retrieving it, never mind calling a number, seems Herculean. For several minutes I can't steady my arm enough for the job. I'm riven with pain, covered in sweat and gasping for air before I finally manage to grab the mobile and rip it from my pocket. Then I rest and the shaking returns, worse than before. I brace myself for another effort, tensing my arms and hands as I begin to attempt to hammer out a text. I keep hitting the wrong keys and drop the phone twice. I'm close to desperate before I'm finally able to gain enough control of my fingers to send the stark message: *HELP*.

Debs phones me seconds later, the fear in her voice unmistakable.

And so it begins. After a lifetime of solitary suffering, the anguish starts to pour out of me, wild and uncontrolled, like air flooding into a vacuum. At first the pressure is too great, and I can't make my meaning clear to her. Debs keeps telling me to slow down, but now that I have finally started, the momentum is irresistible. I say a lot of things in a very short space of time.

Less than an hour later, together we enter the emergency department of a hospital in Belfast. Debs is half a step in front of me, calm and measured as she assumes control of the situation. I'm like a husk behind her, shrunken and diminished. She goes straight to the reception booth and speaks evenly.

'My husband is suicidal. He needs help.'

I'm startled when I hear the words spoken aloud, the admission to strangers of my failure as a person, as a man, as a husband and a father. I tense my body, as if expecting a physical response to the revelation. But nothing happens. All around us are people whose thoughts are occupied with their own problems.

A nurse takes us to a quiet room. He is kind and patient. He explains that a mental health counsellor has been made aware of my situation and will come to see me tonight. It's going to take time; he's at another hospital dealing with another patient. But he will get to me. The nurse is almost apologetic as he explains that he too has other patients that he must attend to, but he promises that he will look in to check on us every now and then. And he does, dropping in for a quick chat when he can, keeping an eye on me. Now the shaking in my hands has been reduced to a slight tremble in my fingers.

We wait for more than four hours. It's well after midnight before the counsellor finally arrives. But by now too much time has passed and I've already begun to disappear back into my shell, convincing myself that nothing is really wrong; that I don't really need to be here; that I'm best trying to deal with it alone. I tell him that I'm feeling better now and suggest that maybe I could go home. But he's patient and insists on talking it through, wanting to know every detail of what happened to me earlier this night.

It's the first time I've spoken to a medical professional about my mental health since my humiliation with the GP two decades earlier. This is very different – the counsellor is sympathetic and clearly isn't judging me. But I still find it hard to unburden myself. I give him some detail, but keep more back, insisting that I'm alright. Eventually he lets me go home, but only after signing me up for a treatment programme and reassuring me that help is there. He gives Debs some phone numbers to call in an emergency. The first light of the morning is already creeping under the curtains before we get home and collapse into bed for a few hours of exhausted sleep.

The following day, things move quickly. In the morning I get a phone call from a social worker. At first, I think she's calling about my welfare but soon realise her main concern is James, who is just four months old. Even in my reduced state, I'm still stung and defensive when she asks if I've ever considered harming my own child. I'm embarrassed at having to assure her that I would never do such a thing.

Next, I have an emergency appointment with a GP in the local health centre. I've never met this woman before, and I have less than ten minutes with her before she has to see the next patient. I tell her a few things, but not much, and she gives me a prescription for antidepressants and sleeping pills before I am dismissed. It's the first time I've ever been given medication to help with what goes on in my head. I'm told that it will take a few weeks before the little tablets begin to work. Then I make myself busy around the house and spend a little time with Debs and James. My son is still small enough that I can hold him in one hand. I sit back in the chair and his little body rests against my chest. I'm content to let him sleep like that for as long as he needs, feeling the rhythm of his breathing.

Later in the afternoon I have to leave the house because I've got an appointment with another counsellor. My case has been deemed serious enough that I've been immediately fast-tracked into a mental health treatment programme. I make a plan with Debs. I'll drive to the appointment before travelling on to visit my Da afterwards. He has been calling to find out how I am. After that, I'll return home for supper and an early night before work tomorrow morning. It's all been figured out. I turn my mobile onto silent and place it in my pocket.

The session with this counsellor goes on for two hours. She tells me to be honest and I try to talk to her about how I'm feeling, how I often can't see a way forward, a way out. How sometimes the pressure of commitments leaves me feeling like I can't breathe. She nods and makes encouraging noises, but I feel like I'm being unfavourably judged. I tell myself that this woman does this for a living – listening to people's problems – but logic seldom works with my brain. I keep just enough of my guard up that she doesn't know just how bad I've allowed things to become. And then I leave and get back into my car. I send a message to Debs.

Just out. Session went well. Going to Da's now. See you soon. Love you xxx.

And then I put my phone back into a jacket pocket and begin to drive in the direction of my Da's house. The events of the past day keep replaying over and over in my head, and this leaves me with an unwelcome sensation of dread. A feeling that I've lifted the lid off something that would have been better left untouched. As I overtake other cars on the road, I'm trying to reconcile contradictory emotions. There's the relief of finally sharing, reaching out for help. But this is smothered by the fear that the way back will be too hard, that I'm nowhere near robust enough for the honesty that is required. I know deep down that I don't believe in the help on offer; I don't think I can be healed.

Suddenly I pull my car to the side of the road and do a U-turn. I begin to drive in the opposite direction to my Da's house. I don't want to talk about it anymore today.

I've no particular destination in mind so I just go in the rough direction of my own house. But I don't intend to go home. Instead, I stop at a pub in the village, pull up a stool at the bar and sip on a pint of stout. The barman tries to begin a conversation about the weather, but I look at him without comprehension and he soon moves awkwardly away. I sit there drinking, intently watching the thick black liquid in the glass diminish. Then I order another pint, allowing it to settle for several minutes before I start drinking again.

Later I leave the bar without a word and begin to walk. It is evening now. There's a lake and a country path at the edge of the village, a spot popular with dog walkers and families. I go there now. It's deserted. I'm struck by how calm the water is, with just an occasional ripple on the surface whenever a duck glides past. I walk around the lake. Then I do it again, and again and again until I've lost count of how many times I've circled the still, black water. The September evening begins to give way to night and soon I struggle to see where I'm placing my feet and I'm guided by the crunch of the stones on the dry, dusty path.

There's a large old tree by the water which has been uprooted and now lies humbled on its side, its great branches overhanging part of the lake, so that some of the leaves and twigs are submerged. Even in the dark I can see the black outline of the hole where the tree once stood, the place where its roots grew before they were pulled clean from the ground. I clamber up onto the huge horizontal trunk and crawl along it away from the edge of the lake towards the deeper water. The bark is rough beneath my hands. I reach the thinner branches at the point which was once the top of the tree, feeling them bend downwards under my weight. I sit on a branch, unsure if it will support me for long. My legs dangle in the dark and my feet go under the black surface. I gasp with shock as I feel the freezing water filling my shoes.

I sit like this, perhaps for a long time. I smoke several cigarettes, throwing the butts into the lake where they remain, floating on the surface. Occasionally I feel myself beginning to lean forward, toward the water, before I rock back again. For a while there are no thoughts or emotions cluttering my mind, and I almost enjoy the liberation of being free of any burden. But eventually I have to admit to myself that I'm not going to do it. Not tonight anyway. As soon as I accept this, I feel the oppression of knowing that I have to be in work in just a few hours. The thought of the dreariness of the ritual and the persistent fear that tomorrow is the day when I'll be exposed as not good enough are enough to send waves of despair through my body.

I start to walk back, my saturated feet squelching on the path. Soon I become disorientated by the depth of the night and wander off the path until I'm stumbling through a field with long, damp grass which snakes around my shoes and clings to the bottom of my trousers. Eventually I find the road which takes me back towards the village and my parked car. Only now do I begin to think about time, how late the hour it is and how long I've been away for. I pull my phone from my jacket pocket and I'm shocked to discover that there are more than 60 missed calls and messages from my wife and family, pleading with me to contact them. The first message I open is from Debs. It reads: *Please come home. We love you xx.* The message reaches something deep inside me, something I had already given up on. I feel shame as I drive home.

***

When I get back, I realise how much trouble I have caused. I've been missing and out of contact for more than seven hours. Coming so soon after my visit to the hospital the previous night, the people closest to me feared the worst. Family have been called to help look for me and the police have been informed that I'm missing and vulnerable.

Friends have had to come to the house to look after James while Debs tries to find me. But now that I have returned, I don't want to talk to anyone; I just want to go to bed. I need to be up for work soon.

I scold my wife for raising such a fuss but she ignores me and phones one of the emergency numbers given by the counsellor last night, and soon I'm placed into a car and driven towards another hospital. I sit with Debs in a bright waiting area in a corridor for what seems like a long time before I'm brought into a small room to meet another doctor. She talks to me for a bit. I tell her I need to be in the office in a couple of hours. She tells me that will not be happening. Then she starts to say something to me, something which sounds a bit legal. At first, I don't follow and I try hard to concentrate on her words. Then the realisation hits that I am being told that she has the power to place me in a hospital. To 'section' me. But she's telling me she doesn't want to have to do that – she wants me to agree of my own free will to be admitted to a psychiatric ward.

I'm about to protest, to tell her that there's been a terrible mistake but Debs, who's been holding my hand throughout, speaks before me.

'I think that might be a good idea. What do you think, Jonny?'

And there's nothing left for me to do but agree. The doctor tells me that she needs to get a second opinion and I'm asked again to wait in the corridor. Months later I will meet this same doctor again as part of my treatment programme, and I will ask her how she came to this opinion. How did she know that something was so badly wrong when I was refusing to engage? She will tell me that, even though I spent a full hour with her that night, I never actually looked at her. That my eyes never once left the floor.

An hour later another counsellor arrives to provide a second opinion. I find myself thinking about the fact that I've now met and spoken to more health professionals in the last 24 hours than in the previous 36 years of my life. This one talks to me for 15 minutes and reads my file. I try to tell her I'm fine, that I just need some sleep, but she concludes that I need immediate hospital treatment. Then, once again, I'm asked to wait in the corridor with Debs while she deals with the paperwork. There are a couple of plastic chairs just outside the office. As we sit there, I can hear her making a call to the staff on the ward, informing them that there's a new patient being sent. But it's the middle of the night and it's creating a lot of fuss for someone. I hear the counsellor trying to placate someone on the other end of the line.

'Yes, I know. . . I understand. . . of course. But trust me, he's a really nice guy. He won't cause you any trouble.'

I almost smile to myself. It seems that I'm just the right sort of the person to be admitted to a psychiatric ward as an emergency case in the early hours. I listen some more. I hear the counsellor use the word 'breakdown' and I'm stung. Until she said the word, it never occurred to me that this might be what is happening to me. I just saw it as another day – granted, a bad one – but just another day.

Then the counsellor comes into the corridor and smiles at us. She tells us everything is set and I can be admitted now. Ward 12, where I'm being sent, is in a separate building in the same hospital. She tells us it is just a five-minute walk across the grounds but she can get someone to come and pick me up if I wish. This question is directed at Debs, who assures her that it's fine – we can find our own way.

We leave the building and begin the short walk towards the ward. The night is warm and the darkness is absolute. My wife has been at my side throughout all of this, but it occurs to me that we have not exchanged any words in a long time. As we walk in the dark towards Ward 12, I turn to her.

'Well,' I begin, 'this is a diabolical development.'

There's nothing for a second, before I hear some low laughter from her. I begin to laugh as well. All other emotions are spent. There's nothing left to do except laugh.

Debs takes me to a door with the electronic lock. She says some words into an intercom and I'm buzzed in. Debs doesn't come too – she's been told that I'll likely be in for a few days and so she has to go home to pick up some clothes and supplies. On the other side of the door, I'm met by a nurse. She speaks to me with a Scottish accent.

Part Two

Eight

'Clean off my Onion . . .'

March 2014

I climb the stairs as I've done thousands of times before. Always the stairs, never the lift – 112 steep steps. I count them off as I inch my way up the three flights, brushing a hand along the red metal bannister. The bannister gets an occasional coat of paint when a VIP comes to the building. Today the paint is coming off in dry flakes in my hand, exposing the dirty rust underneath.

Often it can be a drag getting to the top, the ascent leaving me slightly out of breath and making the muscles in my calves and thighs protest. But today the journey is passing too fast. Today I want to keep climbing without ever reaching my destination. The palms of my hands are warm and damp, so I run them along the sides of the jacket of my new grey suit.

It's my first day back at work. The first time I've returned to the office since my breakdown and hospitalisation six months earlier. After dozens of hours of counselling and the ingestion of countless pills, I'm here to try again. To look my colleagues in the eyes. But as I lay awake the night before, a thought troubled me: *what will I say to them?* Their boss has been away and they're going to want to know why; they are journalists, after all. Some of them may have already heard part of the story, others will have made up their own truths – but how do you tell this story to people you've worked with for years? People who look to you to make the decisions. And there's another thought: *will I have any authority left?*

I'd searched for a precedent. I remembered reading that after a period of mental illness, the author Evelyn Waugh decided to be so open about his condition that he went around asking people: 'Did you hear? I've been absolutely mad! Clean off my onion!'

It's a lovely sentiment but I'm not sure I've got enough chutzpah to pull that off. I hope that, if people ask where I've been, I'll simply have the courage to tell them the truth. I'd like to be able to meet their inquiring gaze and tell them that I was placed in a psychiatric ward after being judged as a suicide risk due to severe depression and anxiety. That I was discharged and I've been recovering since, trying to piece back together my shattered confidence. I'd like to stand in front of them and face down any notion of stigma about mental illness. To make the point that it's nothing to be ashamed of, not a sign of weakness. We'll see.

Up until now I've been able to hide away in my house, any knowledge of my illness confined to my family, doctors and a few very close friends. Cradled snugly in their gentle and loving support, perhaps I got a little bit too comfortable with the time off. The days of family time, easy outings to coffee shops, chats with sympathetic counsellors who kept telling me how much progress I was making. I've slipped away from the real world: the conferences, budgets and deadlines. Even when a return to work was suggested, the planning process unfolded gradually, as slowly as a seed breaking through the soil. The day I went to the company doctor and told him I was feeling better, he congratulated me, helped to draw up a 'return-to-work' plan and then signed me off for another four weeks to allow me to get used to the idea.

But here I am now at the top of the stairs, with my hand on the handle of the heavy double doors. I pause. It's the same journey I took 15 years earlier when I first walked into the newsroom as a young and scared trainee newspaper reporter. I can't remember but I suppose I must have felt as bad then as I do now, the same burning sickness in the depth of my stomach; the internal voice that keeps telling me to turn around, to run away before anyone sees me.

But all those years ago I had pushed my way through the door, fortified by a desire to make my name in a daily newspaper. I had built my career in this large open-plan room, rising swiftly through the ranks, taking on more and more responsibility. I had met my wife in this room and made several friendships which will stay with me for life. I had written hundreds of stories in this room, edited many more, argued over front-page headlines, interviewed politicians and annoyed celebrities with my questions. I had watched over the years as a once great and powerful print industry had weakened and withered. In this same room I had struggled, as had my colleagues, against the inevitable changes that the internet had brought to the news industry. In this room I had found my community, and felt that I was part of something bigger than myself. Here I'd been able to push the worst parts of my own personality so deep inside myself that I sometimes dared to hope I'd be able to keep them permanently buried. But it was also in this room that I had worked myself into a state of mental and physical exhaustion, where I had created an unhealthy attachment to my role and subjected myself to pressures which unleashed the darkest extremes of my mind.

I pause now at the heavy double doors. And then I push them open and enter the bright newsroom. There's the familiar buzz of phone chat, orders being barked and low conversation, so nobody notices me at first. I walk steadily to my desk, right in the middle of the room. It's part of a long body of tables which make up what is known, ridiculously, as the command desk, the gathering point for senior staff who make the decisions which ensure the paper gets out every day. Sitting down, I start to fumble at my computer – but what was once so familiar now seems alien, and the keys feel lumpy and strange below my fingertips. I stare at my screen – there's nothing much there to see but it seems a better option than looking at what I'm sure are inquiring faces all around.

I'm typing something when I'm approached for the first time. A reporter is coming towards my desk. She's one of the newer members of staff, a young thin woman who sometimes struggles to be heard above the din of the room. I hired her myself, poaching her from a small weekly newspaper because I was impressed with her writing skills and her natural intuition about what makes a good story. I had spent a lot of time in the months before I was put into hospital trying to help her to build her confidence, to be robust enough to survive in the brutal news environment. I meet her eye and brace myself for the first of the questions. She leans close.

'It's good to have you back, Jonny.'

That's all. I flush, an instinctive reaction to the unexpected kindness, and mumble some sort of thanks.

***

It's later the same day. The office is quieter now, the productive buzz from earlier has been replaced by a languid silence. Many of the staff have gone home and much of the energy has leaked from the room. The news agenda has slowed to a crawl and the paper is limping towards deadline. I'm working on filling small holes on news pages with weak stories. It's like doing a jigsaw puzzle.

This is the sort of work that I have to do for the moment, according to my 'return-to-work' plan, a written contract agreed between Human Resources and the company doctor. I'm not supposed to be placed in any position of stress. I'm not allowed to make any editorial decisions or to assume any leadership role. Not for several months at least. I'm only supposed to work for four hours each day, which means I'm due to go home in ten minutes.

The plan has succeeded. I'm completely relaxed. And utterly flat and bored. There's a tiny space at the bottom of a back news page which I want to fill before I go home. I'm searching through various electronic baskets and feeds full of written stories but I can't find anything suitable for the small space: I don't want to throw away anything too interesting on such a minor slot. So instead, I start to look through emails, scanning for something which I can turn into a four-paragraph filler. I'm reading through a list of catchlines when something makes me stop. Buried in the list I see something which could be a story, something that we haven't picked up on. *That's a good line*, I think to myself. I look quickly at the news websites, the competition – nobody else has picked up on it yet. For a moment I try to put it out of my mind and concentrate instead on what I'm supposed to be doing. But soon I go back and read the email again. *That's a good line.*

I sit back in my chair and look around the room. My four hours are complete.

Suddenly I get up and call a couple of reporters over to me, surprising them out of their early evening complacency. Soon I'm snapping out orders about what we need to do – who to phone, what to ask, what quotes we need. I talk to the picture desk guys and tell them what photographs I want. It's still too quiet, so I begin stomping around the room, encouraging and cajoling everyone: 'Come on guys, let's get moving! Let's own it! Let's make this our big hit!'

'Our big hit'. Because that's what it's about now, picking our main story for tomorrow morning's paper and making sure we do it better than anyone else. I phone the editor, just to let him know what's happening, but I'm driving it now.

Then I see a text on my phone from Debs: *Are you coming home?* I reply immediately: *On my way*. But I know I'm going nowhere, not until I've seen this through. I tell the production staff that we're clearing the front and two inside pages. There's a small grumble of protest because those pages had already been finished, but I swat it away. This is the plan now.

And I'm enjoying it, the feeling that I'm about to make something happen. This is what I do best. The earlier terror is now a strange, disconnected memory. There's a hum of activity building in the room now. One of the reporters tells me that she can't get the person she needs to talk to on the phone, but I tell her to keep trying and suggest some alternative options. Another reporter is carrying out an interview on the phone but I don't like what I'm hearing, so I catch his eye and begin to scribble better questions on a page of his notebook. Soon I'm on the phone myself, gathering quotes and information. I'm relentless, making constant calls until I get what I need. I make a quick list in my notebook of what I want for the package. A night lead, backgrounder, timeline, Q&A, opinion. Then I start to sketch out an idea for the new front page. The headline, photograph, subhead and plugs. Keeping it simple, direct and powerful. Thinking of the reader.

I'm handing out the instructions but I can't settle so I go back to my computer and begin to go through the pages of tomorrow's edition on the screen – the work already done from earlier in the day which, according to Human Resources, I'm not supposed to look at. I'm reading intros, headlines, captions, whole articles and I soon begin to find things I don't like. The reporter hasn't picked the best line or has been too timid. Clumsy sentences, narratives which don't flow, dozens of words which just don't need to be there. I start to change things, editing every story again, until the pages are starting to resemble something that I can take pride in.

My new front page is under construction but the proposed headline still isn't working. I roll my seat up alongside the production editor and we have a mini-conference, throwing around a few new ideas, laughing at our mistakes. We keep going until we have a headline that fits. Then we change it. And again. We keep working on it because we know it's the one thing we have to get right.

Soon we have a dozen front pages printed and laid out in front of us on the desk, and we're arguing over which is the best one to use. It's approaching our midnight deadline when we finally sign off the front page, sending it with a flamboyant click of the mouse to the printing presses downstairs. There's a feeling of relief mixed with a little sense of triumph, because we know we've created something which will stand out on the shelves when the newsagents open in the morning. I have the personal satisfaction of knowing I've made the thing better, that I've made a difference.

The night-time staff are beginning to drift away but I hang on, unwilling to let go of it all just yet. I check my phone – it's after 1.00 a.m. My four-hour shift has drifted beyond nine hours. I see I've got missed calls and messages from Debs. Only now do I think about how I had promised her that things would be different. How I spent months working out how I could change; how I could find a better balance.

It's taken just one day for me to discover that everything is exactly the same as it has always been.

Nine

The Panic Attack

September 2014

I'm sitting on a toilet. In a cubicle in the gents of a fancy hotel in London. But I'm not taking care of any natural business. Even though my bowels are twisted and in turmoil, I've no thought of relieving myself. The seat is closed and my trousers are fastened. And I'm hiding.

I'm watching my palms with a terrible fascination, holding my hands out in front of me as if they've just grown from stumps tonight. When I think I'm close to mastering my emotions, there's just the hint of a tremble in the fingers which I've chewed until they are bloody and raw. When the panic rolls over me like the tide on the sand, there's a conspicuous shaking which threatens to spread up my arms and take over my whole body. When this happens, I place my hands under my legs until it passes.

There are other people in the area outside my cubicle. I can almost hear them chatting over the low roar of the hand dryer. And I'm certain they must be talking about me. I imagine what they're saying. 'Where did they find that guy?'; 'Did you see the state of him?' I think I hear a mocking, drunken laughter and I feel my face reddening and tears in my eyes, gathering into heavy drops of shame. I try harder to listen but doors keep opening and taps running and I just can't make out the words. But I know it must be about me.

I'm at a conference, an industry event attended by media professionals from all over the UK. I'm here to represent my company, to meet new people, to learn about the latest trends in the business, and what the future holds for all of us. Although nobody said it to me, I guess I've been sent here as a treat, an easy passage back to responsibility after my sickness and time in hospital. And I have tried, I really have. I didn't just head straight for the toilet. I gave it a go. I went to the workshops and the meetings earlier, I tried to force myself into conversations, into groups of people who I don't know. But my voice was never quite loud enough to be heard. I was left with the awful, familiar sense that there must be a secret to easy conversation that all the others in the room bar myself have been let in on. The exhausting loneliness of always feeling that every other person is part of the same club, and that I don't belong.

Earlier that evening, I'd put on the rented evening suit for the gala dinner, the black blazer with the shining buttons and the bow tie. But what had looked smart and stylish back home when my wife was standing next to me now just seemed absurd, hanging off my skeletal frame as I examined myself in the mirror. I'd gone to the drinks reception where everyone was gathered in groups of two or three, all enjoying themselves and chatting merrily. I walked around, feeling the little confidence I had left trickling out of me like grain from a small hole in a sack. When anyone made eye contact or attempted to smile in my direction, I looked down and walked on awkwardly. And so I'd started to drink, glass after glass of red wine. But any power that alcohol ever had to cover up my inadequacies had dissipated many years back. Since then, it has just made things worse, amplifying the dark thoughts and fears which paralyse my mind. And yet I continue to drink, searching desperately for that elusive place where I'll be comfortable, where it all makes sense.

When it was time to assemble for dinner, I'd found my table in the large dimly lit room, full of managers and editors, all of them loud and brash. I was barely noticed as I took a seat and spent several minutes rearranging the cutlery and ripping the paper napkin until it looked like it had been through a shredding machine. I didn't dare to instigate a conversation, so I waited until the stout, balding man on my left turned in my direction. We had a brief, tortured discourse during which he asked where I worked, and then, 'Do you golf?' But after a short time, he quickly and definitively shifted back in the other direction and resumed a conversation with the woman in the red dress on that side. Within seconds the two of them were laughing conspiratorially at some shared remark and I knew that he had said something to her about me.

I sipped some more wine until the smaller, quieter man on my right turned to me. He was easier to talk to, not so brash and forceful. I nodded as he told me about his wife and children and his job. Then he launched into a long anecdote which I struggled to follow, something about a holiday to Malaysia and a day trip on a boat. I was smiling and nodding, laughing at what I imagined might be the right moments, but my brain found it hard to give meaning to all of his words. He was so close, leaning into my face, that I could feel the warmth of his stale, alcohol-infused breath. He finished the story but I didn't quite realise quickly enough and there was an awkward moment of silence which I then rushed to fill with a forced laugh. He looked slightly disturbed and I forced myself to talk before I knew what I was going to say.

'Yes, I know what you mean, a similar thing happened to us on holiday once—'

But he had already turned away and couldn't hear me. Or didn't want to. I flushed and looked around the table to see if anyone else had picked up on my social clumsiness. I gulped some more wine, just to kill another minute. Courses of food came and went, the aromas enough to make me nauseous. Several times I found myself apologising to waiters for uneaten dishes when they asked me if I was finished. Then there were speeches from a little stage at the front of the room and I applauded along with everyone else, without knowing why I was doing it.

I'm not sure exactly what made me flee, what pushed me from a general sense of hopelessness into full-scale panic. Perhaps it was a look from another diner, a misunderstood smile or laugh, an eyebrow raised at the wrong moment. Perhaps it was nothing specific at all – but the numbness in my hands, the cold tingle in my spine and the sweat high on my head all told me I had to get out; that I was in real danger of completely falling apart here in front of a table of strangers. I could already anticipate the unbearable shame of people finding out that there's something wrong with me. That I'm just not right in the head.

So I rushed from the room, bumping against people and walls as a dizziness overwhelmed me, making the room spin so the roof became the walls and the walls were the floor. I burst into the bright bathroom, praying and pleading to the god I don't believe in that a cubicle would be free. The first two doors were locked but the third gave way and I collapsed onto the toilet seat, just managing to lock the door before tears and a long series of anguished gasps of despair escaped from my core.

***

And I've been like this ever since, sitting on this toilet for maybe half an hour, maybe longer. As I said it's a nice hotel, so the bathroom is clean. Or it seems clean until I start to focus obsessively on my physical surroundings. Then I see the grime which has crept into the dark corners of the cubicle, the grains of dirt in the space between the tiles, the wiry, curling pubic hairs stuck to the damp floor, the shit-stained crumpled fragments of toilet paper which have missed the bowl.

Soon I'm repulsed by everything around me and I want to avoid touching anything with my skin. I pull the sleeve of the jacket down over my fingers so I can block direct contact, and I hold my breath, unwilling to breathe any of the now noxious air. I begin to examine every little cream-coloured tile on the wall, fascinated by the regular rectangular shapes, counting how many fill the space from floor to ceiling, searching for any individual slab which is different, any tiny crack or imperfection. I'm filling my thoughts with the inane to squeeze out the fear.

I pull out my phone, partly to give my rampaging mind another diversion, partly to check the time. If it's late enough I could call a taxi and escape. I'm both excited and appalled by the idea, the potential of relief balanced by the daunting new set of challenges the process would present. I see there's a message. I push a few buttons – it's from my wife back home.

Hi honey. James is sleeping soundly. Are you having fun? Are you ok? Xxx.

There's the unmistakable hint of concern in the text and, as ever, I move to quash it immediately, disturbed by the idea that anyone might be worrying about me. Automatically I text back.

Hi Sweetie, I'm fine. All good here. Kiss James for me. Love you xxxx.

I watch as the message leaves my phone and I keep staring at the screen for some seconds after. The familiarity of the process has calmed me a little, slowing my breathing. But then the door moves, shaking the frame of the cubicle and sending me into a new and deeper state of terror. Someone is trying to get in. I stare at the little metal lock which is straining under the pressure.

'Oi!', the accent is from the north of England and the tone unmistakably drunken. 'Oi! Open the door – have you died in there?'

I open my mouth but no words come. Instead, I experience a panic that scrambles any attempt at communication. My bow tie feels like a noose choking air from my body and I'm aware my white shirt is now soaked with sweat. My heart is pounding so uncontrollably fast that I fear it might explode inside my chest. There's another rough knock on the door and I find myself pushing my body further up on the toilet, away from the door, as if trying to escape, to blend into the wall behind me. The door of a neighbouring cubicle opens and I hear the intruder turn away in that direction, grumbling inebriated complaints.

There's the constant murmur of people coming and going in the room, and I know I've trapped myself here, that there's no way out without walking past them. Now the very act of opening the toilet door seems filled with an absurd symbolism, as it separates and protects me from the rest of the world. I think about how much better I've been since I was discharged from hospital. But how the psychiatrist had also warned me not to think that I'd been cured, and that there were bound to be more bad days to come. The inevitability of the relapse. I try all the tricks I've been taught – the breathing, the counting, telling myself that the thoughts are not reality, just my perception of it. But such logic is impotent and pathetic against the full, terrible potency of my mind when it's like this. The dark feelings and fears come so fast and thick, like hailstones bouncing off a dry road. Amid the storm there are little shards of clarity, thoughts that come again and again. *I don't want to live like this. I can't go on like this. I'm tired of always being scared.*

All I want is some relief, relief of any kind. My body is twisted and tight like a rope, making muscles everywhere ache. I've been tensed up for such a long time that I need to let go. Suddenly I relax and my torso and limbs go limp. I feel myself sliding off the toilet, towards the ground and I don't do anything to stop it; I've got no fight left in me. I feel the side of my head bump off the hard floor, but if it is painful, I don't notice or react. I lie very still on the ground. My face is sensitive to every bump and contour of the floor and its shining coldness feels wonderful against my skin. I don't even bother about the particles of dirt sticking to my lips and cheek. I can see underneath the toilet door now, watching pairs of black shoes going back and forth, stopping and starting to walk. I find myself wondering what the name is for that little circle of clear plastic that holds the ends of shoelaces. I think there's a word for it. As I watch the shoes, I think about how tired I am. So tired. I'll just lie like this for a little while. . .

Ten

The Beach

April 2015

My jeans are damp. I've no idea how long I've been sitting on this spot. On these cold, black rocks. It seems like a long time. My legs are hanging limp over the sharp edges, which cut into my legs. The waves are lapping at my boots, darkening the ankles of my jeans. I've been at this place before – countless times, probably hundreds. It's one of my favourite spots on earth. Pale sand which stretches on and on until it fades into wild, yellow grass. But it's the rocks which have always fascinated me the most. Their rugged, wild shapes. Depending on your mood, they can appear sinister and angry or placid and reassuring.

Many times I've sat here. Finding patterns in the outlines of the stones, imagining how the waves have shaped them over the centuries. Even the most solid formations wear away with the constant pressure of time. It's one of the most beautiful places I know. And there's not another person within miles. It's perfect for my business today.

Yes, I've been here hundreds of times. And this will be the last time. I've thought about this moment for most of my life – now it has arrived. This seems to be the right location, appealing to some sense I have of the mystical importance of place.

I lean forward a little and peer into the water, but it's too dark for me to see the bottom. All I have to do is lift myself up and slide off the rock, and all the pain goes away. The endless torture, the blackness of the days. The truth is, I'm just tired of being scared all the time. Nobody can say I haven't tried. I've taken the pills; I've been in hospital; I've talked to the shrink, the counsellors. I've stopped smoking, started exercising, changed my diet. I've tried meditation, mindfulness, behavioural therapy. I've done it all. Once I was allowed to leave hospital, I had to rebuild the wreckage of a life, as a parent, a husband, a professional. Nothing would ever be quite the same because now everybody knew I wasn't invulnerable. The stitching of the cloth had unpicked a little.

So I decided I would be better. Stronger. A better husband, a better father, a better journalist. I would simply work harder at everything in my search for perfection. The day I returned to work was one of the toughest of my life. The macho culture of the newspaper industry does not sit well with this sort of vulnerability. I knew there would be rumours about where I had been, why I had been away. But soon I was back helping to run the place and it was as if I'd never been away. If anything, I was even louder than before, even more severe. As if I had to prove something to others. And to myself.

So the weeks went on as before. And then during the London trip, the dark feelings returned. The heaviness, and the fear have been with me ever since – and now I just can't do it anymore. It's bad enough to fall in life. But when you fall, admit you're not strong enough, do everything they tell you to, get back up – and then you fall again – that's the most crushing failure. The utter demoralisation of trusting the system, raising your own hopes, waking up in the morning and thinking, 'I can do it!' – only for it all to fall to pieces again. None of it works; there is no help; it doesn't get any better. This is the way it's always going to be... *Unless you do something about it.*

So here I am, sitting on the rocks, watching the waves below, their foam rising off the surface. I've always had a fascination, an obsession, with this – how it is not to be anymore. Not to feel, not to think, not to care, not to love. It's at once terrifying and compelling – like a tragic scene that you can't look away from.

I shiver a little and check my watch. I'm supposed to be at work now. It won't be long before I'm missed, before the questions start. I light a cigarette. I said I'd quit smoking – but, well, it doesn't really matter anymore. I take out my mobile. My link to every other part of society; the networking tool that binds us all to each other. I drop it into the water. There's barely a splash as it sinks soundlessly to the bottom. I almost smile at the corny melodrama of the gesture. Even now I can't resist the urge to turn things into a grand narrative. A neat story. But that's not important anymore. I shift my position, as if to move forward. But I don't. I wait a few minutes. My mind is not as clear as I imagined it would be. I smoke another cigarette. I go to move forward again. But still, nothing happens.

My first thought is about my own cowardice. I'm managing to fuck this up as well. But this now isn't fear – it's something different. A feeling, almost like a force stopping me from going ahead. Of course, I think about my family at this moment: what it will be like for them? But, the truth is, when your mind is this diseased, you are able to get round that question. It's easy to convince yourself that the ones you love will be better off without you; to tell yourself that you don't want to mess up your child the way you messed up yourself. But no, as I'm sitting here paralysed on this rock, the truth is that my feelings are about myself. It's some kind of instinct which is holding me back. It's impossible to define: the best way I can think of expressing it is that it's a belief coming out of my core, which tells me that I've got more to give. That, if there is a purpose to this whole fucking mess, I haven't yet fulfilled it.

And that's the thing which breaks me.

I wasn't crying before, because I didn't feel anything. But now I am. Because if you put your hand deep enough into the driest sand, you can still sometimes find a little bit of moisture. I realise that I haven't completely given up on myself and that what had seemed completely smooth just seconds ago is now rough like the back of my hand. And there's a whole heap of new problems. The anxieties and pressures and fears begin to flood back in ... I'm so weary. How do I kickstart this thing again? I was supposed to be in work an hour ago. Instead, I'm sitting fifty miles away from the office in wet, muddy jeans. I stand up and peer into the dark water. I'm looking for my phone but I can't see it. The small black slab of plastic and metal which connects me with every other person I know in this world – and it's gone. So much for grand gestures.

Then I wipe mud off the arse of my trousers and I begin to walk back along the beach. And, as always, my mind is desperately trying to make sense of it all. To find a point to what has happened. But it's beyond me. So I think I'm going to have to go back to the doctor. Get stronger pills, more counselling. But I'm afraid, because these things didn't work before.

And now a thought I had while sitting on the rocks comes back to my mind: *This is the way it's always going to be. Unless you do something about it.* So now, maybe for the first time, I ask myself why the treatments didn't work. Was it because of my innate, maddening refusal to accept change and to face up to my own vulnerabilities? Yes, I said and did all of the right things, ticked all the boxes. But how much of the process did I actually believe in? How much personal responsibility was I prepared to accept?

I can't be better than I was, I can't be stronger. I've been down that road. And that leaves me with nowhere to go except... Except to be worse, to be weaker. And maybe that's ok. Maybe accepting that is the first step in changing myself. I'm Jonny McCambridge and I'm just not strong enough to cope on my own.

There, I said it. There's a silence. And then the world moves on. I walk back along the beach, seeing lots of things for the first time today. I notice a single, solitary line of footprints in the sand. Footprints which are heading towards the rocks. And now there's another line of footprints, going the other way.

Eleven

Therapy

November 2015

'Think about a traumatic moment in your childhood. Something that still disturbs you today.'

I shift uncomfortably in my chair. And it is a chair – not a couch like you see on telly or in films. Just a black plastic chair in a glass-walled room where a sympathetic middle-aged woman sits opposite me. Tanya is my new counsellor, the latest person tasked with helping me to chop a path through the jungle in my brain in search of answers. The latest person encouraging me to ask, why? Why do I react to people and situations the way I do? Why do I make the decisions that I do? Why am I always afraid?

As I think about the question, she chews on the end of a biro and stares at some scribbles in a notebook.

A traumatic moment in my childhood? 'OK,' I say finally, 'Brazil getting knocked out of the 1982 football World Cup. I still think about that nearly every day.'

Tanya looks up quickly. I presume this is to see if I'm making fun of her, but my expression is completely earnest. She's confused. I could tell her about how I had cried for hours after the flamboyant Brazilian side were eliminated from the tournament more than three decades ago, by the organised, ruthless, but dull Italians. I could tell her about how I have lain awake on hundreds of nights, obsessing about what happened during a game that took place when I was just seven years old; about how it could have been different, should have been different. I could tell her how I was thinking about that match just this morning as I was changing my son's nappy. I could tell her all of this, but I sense it's not the moment.

'Alright,' she says, 'let's try something else. You said your parents split up. What do you remember about that day?'

I wince at the question and Tanya smiles encouragingly. But my reaction is not from pain at the memory. I'm wincing because I know I'm about to give her another answer that she'll hate. But I made a promise to myself before I came here today. That I'll answer the questions honestly. That I won't just say what I think she wants to hear, or give the answer that most sounds like the sort of thing a person with chronic depression might say. I won't just say the thing that might make it easy for her to tell me that I'm making good progress, or that I think will make her like me, or feel sorry for me. Since my day sitting on the rocks at the beach, I've been trying with new energy to make this process work.

So I'll give the answer which reveals exactly what was going on in my mind on the day my parents split up – even if it makes me sound like a bastard.

I begin. 'Well, it was April 1996. . . The Masters is always played in April.'

I notice Tanya's uncertain look.

'The golf tournament – The Masters at Augusta,' I clarify. 'It happened on the Sunday, the final day. Da had left and Ma was crying and the golf was on the telly. Greg Norman had a six-shot lead over Nick Faldo and he blew it. He'd never won a major in America and he'd never have a better chance than this. I remember him going into the water on the twelfth. Then he missed a chip on the fifteenth and he sank to his knees. The look on his face . . . I just felt so sorry for him. There was all this drama and anguish going on at home, but all I could think about was the haunted look on Norman's face that evening – I'll never forget it.'

The answer hangs there between us. Tanya is watching me carefully, reading my expression. She scribbles something else on the pad and then gives me another warm smile.

'OK, Jonny, we've made really good progress today. Let's pick it up again next week.'

I leave the room and walk down a corridor, which reminds me of school. There are posters on the walls promoting services, helplines, support groups. I step outside the clinic. My car is close by but I decide to walk for a bit; I'm agitated and I need to think it through. The last thing Tanya said is going around in my head. *We've made really good progress today.* I'm angry at myself because I promised to be honest and I know what I should have said, *No Tanya, we haven't made any fucking progress at all.* I'm as far away as ever from understanding why I am the way I am.

And it's been this way for two years now. A series of psychiatrists, counsellors, therapists and experts, scores of hours of talking, analysing and sharing – and I haven't taken a single step in the direction of greater understanding. And it's not because there's been any lack of effort. A large number of people have given a large amount of time to trying to help me. I've opened myself up more than I ever thought possible. I've sat in front of strangers and wept as I told them of the times I've come close to killing myself; shared with them the utter emptiness and desolation of my soul in the middle of the night. I've discussed being a father, a husband and a journalist. I've talked about my childhood, my upbringing, my relationship with my Ma and Da, their relationship with each other, my siblings, school friends and girlfriends. I've talked about my job and the future, where I'd like my life to be in a few years' time, all my hopes and fears for my son. I've done relaxation, meditation, breathing, and a whole array of exercises designed to train my mind to work in a different way. I've been made aware of the physical workings of my brain, what the different parts do, and which of these are most affected by depression. There have been some good sessions and some very, very bad sessions.

But throughout it all, any sense of understanding myself has remained frustratingly elusive. The more that I have accepted and confronted my illness, the more questions have arisen and the less likely it has seemed that I will find answers to them. How can I expect other people to understand when I can't make sense of it myself? Keyhole surgery doesn't work on the mind – you can't simply go in there and locate what's gone wrong.

Looking for the origin has proven futile. My childhood was unremarkable. Yes, my family were often distant from each other and my parents had an unhappy marriage, but that was hardly unusual in rural Northern Ireland in the 1970s. I was a shy and sensitive adolescent, and I remember long periods of unhappiness and loneliness at school and at home but I'm not aware of any specific trigger which first led me to consider taking my own life. For as long as I can remember I've always been a worrier, and if I didn't have something to worry about for myself, I would worry for somebody else. As an adult, as my personal and professional lives become more stable, I found myself becoming more afraid and miserable at exactly the time when I should have been relaxing into an easier existence.

The other possibility is that it's just a malfunction of my brain – perhaps some genetic vulnerability or faulty neurological wiring up there? Maybe my hippocampus has become shrunken and shrivelled as a result of decades of miserable thoughts and feelings of self-loathing? In the past two years I've been prescribed a long series of antidepressants, little pills with long names, to supposedly regulate my moods and stimulate certain chemicals in my brain. I wasn't concerned about any stigma around going on medication – instead, I was hugely relieved and excited, because I'd met so many people who told me that medication had changed their lives, that they can look to the future with hope and promise, as long as they've got their tablets. 'Just take the little pill and it all makes sense,' they seemed to be saying.

So I took my first antidepressant and I waited for something to happen, for me to feel differently. I was told it would take time. I waited months without any noticeable difference in my mental state. Then my doctor changed my medication and we went through the same process again. This was to happen several times. I've been taking pills for a long time without knowing how much they are helping me, although there's a part of my mind which wonders if I'd be worse without them. It's difficult to be sure.

As I start yet another lap of the mental health clinic car park now, I light a cigarette. It occurs to me that each person's thought processes are unique and therefore any understanding and treatment of mental illness must be individually tailored. Perhaps it's just luck that allows the professionals to stumble upon a method which works with a patient and so in my case, the odds of a breakthrough seem longer than ever. I've got half an hour a week with a counsellor, one small white pill every morning and a wallet full of emergency phone numbers in case I get into trouble. It's clearly not enough to dissect and solve the mysteries of my brain.

I find myself thinking that I would need a team of white-coated scientists following me around constantly, watching my every move, writing down each inane utterance, to have any chance at understanding what it's all about. But that's not how it works, the rope is only so long. In today's society this condition is reaching epidemic proportions and there are thousands of people who need help, who deserve help as much as I do. That's just the way it is. There must be a reason why I still get upset about a football game played more than 33 years ago. Or why I felt more sadness about a millionaire golfer failing to win a tournament than I did about my family falling apart. The maddening thing is, I just don't know what it is. I don't know why.

I've got a low feeling as I throw away the cigarette butt and get into my car. I know the understanding has to come from me and I can't provide it. I like Tanya but I can't really see the point of going back to see her again. I know that she can't make me any better. I drive out of the carpark and I'm not sure if I'll come back.

***

It's a few days later, early in the morning and I've come through the agony of another sleepless night. The terror was at its most acute in the dark hours but the dim morning light has brought little relief. I'm no help at home, unable to assist Debs to look after our son or prepare breakfast. I'm not even able to make my wife a cup of tea and this reduces me to tears. She is as understanding as ever, but my feelings of uselessness are adding to my already black mood, piling layers of fresh misery on top of what's already festering. As she busies herself around the house, doing the things that have to be done, I have the feeling of being a burden and it's a weight on my chest which just won't shift.

I go outside for a walk, partly to clear my head and partly to get out from under Debs' feet. I've convinced myself, as I often do, that my family would be better off if I wasn't around. Sometimes exercise can help to moderate some of the impact of an episode of chronic depression, and it's worth a try. I walk on and on, forcing myself to go faster until I'm covered in a film of sweat and my feet ache, but the thoughts are still attacking my mind. There's a little river walk, a path beside the lazy Lagan, overgrown with weeds and wildflowers and strewn with empty beer cans. I walk along the path, then I turn and walk back. I keep walking up and down the same stretch of river, trying to control my thoughts and to kill some hours. Then I check the time and new waves of a panicked sadness rush at me – it's still so early in the morning and I'm not calming down. There's still so long to go in the day and I'm really scared now, because I'm not sure I can get through it feeling this way.

I pull out my wallet and search through cards and scraps of paper. I find what I'm looking for and punch a number into my phone with trembling fingers. It's answered on the third ring.

'Hello?'

'Tanya – it's me, Jonny. I know it's not my day but I really need to talk to someone.'

Less than half an hour later I'm sitting, softly crying, in her waiting room. There are several other people there but I'm long past caring about being a spectacle. I haven't been waiting long when Tanya walks into the room and waves for me to follow her, the usual sympathetic smile on her face. We go to the same room with the windows on both sides and start to talk.

At first there's a lot of me wailing and not many words spoken, but Tanya is patient and gives me time until I'm able to compose myself. Then we talk. We're not solving anything, just talking. At some point, because my mind is now distracted by our conversation, I start to forget that I'm desperate. The feeling of utter hopelessness which was crippling my thoughts has been diluted. A little at first, and then some more. About half an hour later we're actually having a laugh, as I tell some stupid story and Tanya smiles at the details. Then there's a moment of silence. She asks me if I need her to call anyone. I tell her that, no, I'm going to be fine. Today, at least. Then I tell her that I'll see her again next week.

I leave the clinic for the second time in just a few days. I'm quite excited now because I want to see my wife and son, to spend some time with them. I'm looking forward to the rest of the day. There's been no advancement in understanding and I know that I'm not any better than I was before I went in. But just having the chance to have some human contact, a person who was prepared to listen, made the difference today. And sometimes, that's enough.

Twelve

Leaving Work

September 2016

James starts nursery school today. He's a timid and nervous boy, and I know it's going to be difficult for him. There will be tears, he'll be clinging on to Mummy like a limpet to a sea rock, refusing to let go of her at the classroom door. He'll be wiping snot on the sleeve of his new red jumper, his first uniform. It's a hard day for a parent too, one more step in the natural bitter-sweet process of having to let go that little bit more. As my son takes those first faltering steps to independence I want to be there smiling, nodding encouragement; meeting his scared gaze and telling him it's all going to be ok.

But I'm not there to do any of that. I'm in the newsroom, at my desk amid the piles of papers, letters and press releases. The desk where I spend most of my time. I left it too late to ask for the day off, my mind too jumbled to remember the date, and the pressurised reality of life at a daily paper meant that I couldn't be spared today. I have one child, one go at this, one chance to not fuck it up. And on a day when my boy really needs his daddy, I'm at work. I'm always at work. The sense of failure as a father eats away at me.

I'm editing today, so the responsibility for producing tomorrow's edition lies with me. And I'm facing the familiar problems. No front-page story, no front-page photograph, no headline, no editorial concept. A paper full of holes to be filled and I'm struggling to come up with ideas. I swivel slightly in my chair and watch the staff, chatting freely, sharing confidences and having a few giggles. Some are watching the clock to see how long is left in the working day.

I get the all-too-common feeling of envy for those who are able to walk away from it all. Those for whom this is merely a job, not a vocation. I feel the ache of a desire to be free of the responsibility, to be able to simply leave the office and not worry about work until I return the next morning. Then I think about my son in his new red jumper. But I have to quickly force the image out of my mind, as the urgency of the circumstances brings me sharply back to the immediate situation. The staff need direction; people are depending on me making some decisions. I'm bound to this.

I'm working on the intro of a weak story. Staring wearily at my computer screen, my fingers flickering uncertainly over the white mouse. I'm wondering if it can be turned into a front-page lead, if I can jazz it up; find the right line, the headline. A pain behind one of my eyes is troubling me and I don't even notice when a young reporter moves alongside me. I'm staring at my computer as she sits down. I still don't turn to her so she nervously clears her throat to get my attention, the way I might have done when I was starting out two decades back. Then she asks me a question, something inane but well meant, touched by the naivety of inexperience.

It's the wrong moment, there are just too many things to be done and the tasks are already threatening to overwhelm me without adding more. I blurt out some sort of short reply. It should be a warning that now is not a good time to approach me. But the young reporter doesn't pick up on my harsh tone and persists with the inquiry. A shot of anger goes through me. I don't shout, it's quieter than that, more sinister.

'If you want to remain working here, then you'd better not say another word! Get out of my sight!' I hiss.

There are enough people around to hear what's going on and it's awkward for everyone. The young reporter retreats tearfully. I make the decisions that are needed, and we manage to get the paper out.

And that should really have been the end of it. The newsroom can be a harsh environment, particularly when deadline time is looming. I've been on the receiving end myself of countless 'bollockings' over the years, and I know I've handed out a few as well. But there's something about this particular exchange which bothers me and stays with me long after I should have set it aside. It troubles me as I suffer through yet another sleepless night. It's in my head the next morning when James is telling me about his first day at nursery – and I know that I behaved badly.

***

It's a couple of days later. As predicted, James is struggling with the transition to nursery. His sobbing at the classroom door is serious enough to make Debs and me wonder if the whole process is actually causing him harm – if the trauma outweighs the benefit. We spend hours chatting about it, discussing techniques and methods to make it less painful for him, and us.

And of course, work goes on because the paper has to come out every day.

It's another long shift in the office and one of my

colleagues is talking to me; she's says she's concerned about my health and wants to know if I'm coping with the pressure. It's now three years since I was hospitalised in Ward 12. I'm only half-listening to her at first and I brush her worries away. But then she says something which gets my full attention. She mentions my exchange with the younger reporter from earlier in the week. The staff have been talking about it, she tells me – whispering amongst themselves. I'm told that many of them defended me – 'Jonny's been under a lot of stress recently.' But I'm also told that the young reporter involved has been left afraid, and is now too intimidated to talk to me. In fact, she's too scared to enter the newsroom when I'm there. I think about my own son, crying at the door of the classroom, then about this nervous young professional coming to me for guidance. And suddenly a strong feeling of certainty floods into my mind, telling me that I'm finished in this job.

Sometimes, the mind places undue significance on random events. It's a human frailty which, I imagine, afflicts us all. Through our telling and retelling, experiences become slightly tinted to suit a narrative. Sometimes this can take the form of a distortion of the facts, by design or not. On other occasions a chance single occurrence within a chain of events assumes in retrospect the importance of a pivotal moment, a turning point which takes us in what we now see as a pre-ordained direction of travel. Like an autumn leaf dropping from a tree onto the surface of the wide river and then being carried along in the strong current. Maybe that's what has happened to me here.

In truth there is no one single event which leads me to leave work, to derail the career I have been building for 20 years. It has been coming for some time, and the incident with the young reporter is just one grain in a large bag of rice. But it is at the end of this day, after this exchange with my colleague, that I decide to phone my doctor.

'I think I'm in a bad place.'

That's all I need to say. She tells me to come in to see her the next morning. And when I do, I tell her once more about the constant fear, the anxiety which is as familiar as my skin. The suicidal thoughts which are coming back, worse than ever. The long, solitary walks; the nights spent standing on the edge of bridges; the afternoons sitting on the rocks on the beach. I hadn't admitted it to myself yet but I hear myself tell my doctor that I'm afraid I'm going back towards the state which led to me being admitted to Ward 12 in the first place. Then, for the second time in three years, she tells me that I have to take some time off work. But this is different; this time I have the feeling that there is no way back. This time, I'm not immediately plotting how I'll return to the office better than before, dazzling everyone with my powers of recovery. The truth is, I'm tired of it all and I've accepted that something has to change. I can't keep on going like this.

I leave the doctor's surgery and drive home. Sitting alone on the sofa I begin to think about what happens next. My hands and legs begin to shake horribly and my breathing becomes so fast that I'm worried that I'll never be able to control it again.

**

It is James' second week at nursery school. The red jumper is definitely too large. I take his small hand in mine as we walk into the fenced area around the school building. I can feel his body stiffen as we get closer but I know he's trying to be brave for me. Debs has told him that Daddy is feeling poorly and he has to be an extra-specially good boy. I've not been here at the school before and I'm slightly uncertain of where to go, what the routine is – so James takes the lead and guides me. His blue eyes meet mine. 'Don't worry, Daddy, I told Mummy I'd look after you.'

As he says this I have to look away, out into the playground, to maintain my composure. My son's courage holds right until the moment when I hand him over to the teacher. Then he starts to panic and wail and I bend to hug him, telling him repeatedly that it's just for a couple of hours and that I'll be right here to pick him up. A classroom assistant peels him out of my arms and I stand up, dazed and upset.

I walk outside and the teacher follows me. She thinks I look emotional and wants to check I'm ok. A small gesture of humanity. She's from the same part of the country as me and soon we're talking about shared friends. Then she tells me that James is settling into his class really well and that I'm not to worry; it's always a bit tricky at first. I thank her and walk away. I've now got some spare time before pick-up so I go to the little coffee shop beside the school and order something to eat.

Two hours later I'm standing with a large group of parents as the classroom door opens again. Because I'm near the front, James is one of the first to be released and the nursery teacher nods to me, mouthing, 'He's been fine.' My son runs when he sees me and leaps into my waiting arms. I ask him what he'd like to do as a treat and he wonders if we can go to the park where the trains go past. It's a short drive and I'm happy to do it.

Soon I'm pushing him on the swings. He seems to be a little bit confused, perhaps not understanding why I'm here or why I've been spending so much time with him over these past few days.

'Higher, Daddy, higher,' he yells, determined to make the most of it in any case.

I check my watch. It's four o'clock, which is hard-wired into my brain as the time for the journalists' news conference meeting. A tremble of anxiety runs through my body, as if my physical state hasn't quite caught up with this new order of being. Officially I'm off work on medical leave, but I already know that I won't ever go back to the newsroom. As soon as a little crack appeared in my certainty that I would always be a journalist, I was surprised at how quickly it all fell apart; how easily all the years of effort, of progression, were abandoned. How, when I accepted that decision, I felt like my skull had undergone a trephination, such was the release of pressure.

But now there's a new problem. I know I can't go back, but I haven't got a forward direction in mind. I'm aware that I'm in the process of doing something that sounds like the plot of a bad TV drama. Except this is real. I am walking away from a successful career, a well-paid job and stability. It's not a change of direction or even a recalibration of some kind, because I have no alternative plan. It is leaping off the cliff and hoping that the tide is in.

And I don't even know if it is going to help. Take away the familiarity of work, and perhaps the wretched depression and anxiety will be worse. Especially given the new worries about how I'll pay my bills or the mortgage. What happens when the money runs out? How will we buy food or clothes for our son? I think about the future and suddenly I'm even more nervous and afraid. The days stretch out in front of me, empty and tinged with uncertainty.

But then I force myself back to the moment, concentrating on pushing the swing a little higher each time until James is howling with delight. For now, there is no plan beyond spending time with my son, and trying to find a way to heal.

'Daddy, can you get me an ice cream now?'

'Of course I can, son.'

'Can I have sprinkles on it?'

'Yes, you can.'

'And strawberry sauce?'

'OK.'

Standing at the van, it occurs that I probably haven't bought an ice cream like this in years. I'm not quite sure what to ask for and I order a whipped cone which is almost bigger than James' head. He can't quite believe his good fortune, and grasps it with two hands as he strolls alongside me on the path which leads to a green area with the tall trees and the duck pond. He licks eagerly at the ice cream, like a thirsty dog lapping water. But it's too big for him and quickly begins to melt, sending little streams of cold, milky liquid onto his fingers and the sleeves of his red jumper. I think about what Debs told me about keeping his uniform clean.

'Here, give me that, son, it's dripping everywhere. I'll lick it for you.'

Reluctantly he goes along with this but doesn't take his suspicious eyes off me. I lick the ice cream and it's good, so I lick it again. My son bursts into tears.

'Stop, Daddy! You're taking too much! Stop licking the strawberry sauce!'

'Jaysus! I'm only taking a wee lick. Sure, look at the size of it! There's loads!'

We keep walking just like this, arguing over his ice cream. Walking in a new direction.

Thirteen

Facing the Day

October 2016

I'm not asleep but not quite awake either; I'm somewhere between the two. I can hear a noise outside the window – the tortured squeal of the bin lorry as it crushes and compresses piles of rubbish. The sound reminds me of the bray of a distressed animal and I'm repulsed and terrified by it. I shrink down into the bed and pull the duvet over my head to block it out. Soon, more sounds filter through – the low rumble of a passing car and the dog next door barking at the singing morning birds. The bright early autumn sun is pouring through the thin blinds of the room and its rays reach the edge of the pillow, close to my face. It's a fine day and it occurs to me that most people will be getting ready to go to work, or if not, to go out and make the most of the weather. But, for me, I know the first, almost insurmountable challenge will be just getting out of bed, before I can even contemplate facing the world on the other side of the glass.

On the worst days, the mental impacts on the physical. The plodding, suffocating heaviness seems to pour out of my mind and into my bones; the overwhelming sadness morphs into an oppressive weight on my chest. It's not only the fear and anxiety about getting out of bed and going out into the world that afflicts me, it's the fact that I'm not sure I've even got the physical strength to do it. I'm brutally tired, as always, but the relief of sleep is rarely to be found these days. My arms and legs feel like alien limbs, not under my own control.

I feel I've been lying like this for hours and I know that the longer I leave it, the worse it will be. I keep telling myself that I have to try, whispering it over and over to myself like a prayer. I pull my head off the pillow, just a couple of inches at first, before sinking down again like a bag full of wet sand. My skull aches but I will myself on. *Come on, you can fucking well do it!*

I lie there, building up for another effort. This time I manage to lift my head a little higher, heaving my body up somewhere close to a sitting position until I can lean against the headboard. Then I rest again. My arms are folded across my chest, as if I'm holding or protecting myself, and my head is sloping forward into a slow, desperate nod. The urge to slide back down into the bed is vast and threatens to shatter me. *You've nothing to get up for. Why are you putting yourself through it?* I hold myself even tighter until the despair passes.

I feel that if I don't get moving soon then the last splinter of hope for the day will be gone, so I quickly swing my legs sideways until I'm sitting unsupported. The contact of the carpet with my bare feet sends trembles of anxiety up my legs and through my body and, again, the longing to go back rather than forward is fierce. I rest some more, nodding and shivering. The wall is just a metre away so I thrust myself up and forward, unsure if my legs even have the strength to support me. I grab desperately at the wall, scraping and scratching at the plaster until little flecks of paint have wedged themselves underneath what's left of my fingernails. But I'm standing. Slightly bowed rather than straight, but I'm definitely upright. For just a second there's the dimmest glow of triumph, before the thought of the vast emptiness of the day ahead snuffs it out and I'm terribly afraid again.

I move slowly to the bathroom and collapse heavily onto the toilet. Immediately my bowels explode violently below me, sending a spray of thick, rusty water all around the white bowl as I gasp in pain. I almost fall off the toilet, having to put my arm on the bath for support as the twist of cramp sends spasms of agony through my guts. When my stomach settles a little, I move over to the shower, setting the water temperature as hot as I can bear until the steam is rising from the cubicle. I lean my head against the tiles as the hot spray pelts the back of my neck. Then I stop the jet and the cold air shocks me as I open the shower door and grab a towel from the rail, groaning as I bend down to dry the spaces between my toes.

I rub the steam off the mirror with the palm of my hand, leaving ugly streaks on the glass. I'm appalled by what is staring back: the red, puffy features and greying hair; the bearded face creased by worry and desolation; the fear in the eyes. There's still steam in the room and the wet particles cling to the mirror once more, obscuring my view again. This time I don't wipe it off.

I dress in the same clothes I wore yesterday and go downstairs, into the kitchen. The first thing I see is a note on the table from Debs, a sheet of white paper ripped from a notebook. I pick it up. *Hi honey – can you order the heating oil? The number's on the fridge door. I'll be back for dinner. Don't forget to pick James up, love you x.* I set the note back down and fill the kettle.

I'm suddenly hungry but I don't know if I'll be able to eat. I walk around the room, opening and closing drawers and cupboards, moving jars and tins about. Everything seems messy and disorganised – the disarray fills me with hopelessness; the task of bringing order to it all seems insurmountable. No matter how much I do, I'm never able to stay on top of things. I open James' cupboard and find a packet of chocolate-covered biscuits in the shape of animals. I take the biscuits to the table with a hot coffee and sit there without moving for a moment. Then I rip the packet open and start to eat. I tell myself I'll have a couple, just to take the edge off my hunger, but I keep going, my jaws metronomic as I stuff one after another into my mouth.

Soon I've gone past the point of being hungry or experiencing any enjoyment in the process – but I keep gorging myself. I start to feel ill but I continue, pushing yet another biscuit into my mouth while I'm still chewing the previous one. I keep doing this this until they're all gone and then I use the back of my hand to wipe crumbs from my lips. I steady myself, fighting off the urge to vomit. Then I go to the fridge where the phone number of the oil delivery company is pinned. I take the scrap of paper back to the table and lift my mobile. I look at the number and slowly type the first couple of digits into the phone, my fingers trembling. Then I drop the mobile and go into the back garden for a smoke. I quit once again a few months back and I've managed the abstinence pretty well, but unbeknownst to Debs, I still keep some cigarettes in the house for times like these.

I walk round in circles on the paved area, taking long draws of nicotine as I try to build myself up for the ordeal of making the call. I consider how a few months back I was running a newspaper, while now I'm too afraid to make a phone call to order oil. Several times I go back into the kitchen towards the phone but each time I retreat to the safety of my back yard.

Eventually I manage to get the complete number dialled but the first sound of the ring tone is like an electrical shock to my head and I hang up and walk away again. The next time, I get as far as hearing a voice on the other end of the line before I cut the call. I sit down but stand up almost immediately, feeling heat and drops of sweat on my brow and the back of my neck. I will myself on. I redial again, holding the small black phone in two hands to control the trembling. The voice which answers sounds harsh and impatient to my ears. I immediately think I'm being judged.

'Hello?'

The voice is so severe that my resolve swiftly begins to fracture. I try to speak but no words come. My breathing starts to speed up.

'Hello! Is there anyone there?'

I grasp the phone tighter, pushing it into the side of my face so hard that I can feel its electronic warmth. I force myself to stay on the line. *Come on, come on!*

'Yes, yes, I'm sorry . . . um. . . I just wanted to order some home heating oil.'

The conversation passes a little easier after that and the transaction is finished in minutes. This time when I hang up, there's a little pulse of triumph somewhere in my brain, the contentment of knowing that I've achieved something in the day, and that I can, after all, impose my will on the worst parts of my own personality. I quickly rattle out a text message which I send to Debs: *Ordered the oil, love you x.*

I want to keep going now, to push myself to see what else I can get done today. I begin to think about dinner, not as a burden but as a challenge to master. Concepts of dishes I could make roll through my brain, the ideas coming quicker than I can process them. I'll surprise Debs by making a big effort, preparing a proper meal from scratch, perhaps with a bottle of wine and a bunch of flowers as well. We'll get James down to bed and then have a perfect night together, talking and laughing.

I pull on a light jacket, grab my wallet and leave the house, noticing the warmth of the sun on my face. The little shop is just around the corner and I'd sooner walk than drive. I use the time to think about what I'll cook and begin to prepare a shopping list in my mind, trying to put the items in an order that I'll remember. It occurs to me that I'm looking forward to the rest of the day.

It's when I turn the corner of my street and the shop comes into view that my courage begins to fail. I notice the car park is busy, with a number of vehicles queuing to get a space. I walk closer until I can see through the front window. There's a line of customers snaked around the shop, some carrying baskets or trying to control bored children. All I can read in the faces of these shoppers is impatience and anger. Two men, dressed like farmers or builders with heavy boots, dirty jeans and thick tanned arms, are talking animatedly in the front doorway. They're probably fifteen feet from me but I can hear every word of their coarse conversation and their rough, throaty laughter jars against my brain.

There's only one spot left in the car park and two motorists want it. When one car moves into the space, the driver of the other shouts and waves her arms in exasperation.

I've reached the front of the shop now but I can't remember what I've come for. The two men move aside to let me enter but I don't go in, instead I quickly turn back towards the car park. I know they'll be watching, wondering what's wrong with me, so I drop my eyes to the ground and quicken my pace. I'm too anxious to pay attention to my surroundings and I almost collide with a reversing car, leading the driver to sound an angry blast of the horn, which sends me into a deeper panic. I'm almost running as I move further away from the shop. I don't know where I'm going – I just know that I have to get away.

Fourteen

'Will you be ok on your own?'

January 2017

I stand in the doorway, in my pyjamas, and kiss Debs and James goodbye. She's dropping him at day care before going to work. James goes to a crèche three days a week before and after nursery school. Even though I'm at home all day now, Debs and I still think part-time childcare is a good arrangement because it gives him a chance to meet lots of other children and improve his social skills. We're hoping that this will help to make the switch to primary school – which isn't so far away in the future now – a little easier, because it means he'll already have some pals who'll be making the transition with him.

So, with no work to go to and no plan for life, I'll have time to myself today. Too much time. There's a fleck of concern in my wife's eyes.

'Will you be ok on your own?' she asks.

'Of course I will,' I shoot back immediately, smiling to reassure her and to cover my own offended impatience at the question.

'And will you maybe change out of your pyjamas today?'

'Uh-huh.'

'If you get a chance, will you go to the barber? Your beard is getting a bit wild.'

'Yes, honey.'

'And can you remember to pay the window cleaner?'

'Uh-huh.'

I wait until I see her car disappearing around the corner before I turn back inside. I notice my reflection in the large, rectangular mirror in the hallway and smooth down some grey hairs on my chin. It's now been over three months since I left the paper. If I imagined that the amputation of my career would instil new motivation and energy into my life, then it has not been the case. Instead, with the removal of the structure and discipline of the office routine, I've rapidly retreated further away from society.

For a few days after my departure was announced, I was swamped with calls and messages of goodwill from friends and former colleagues. But they quickly dried up and now, I've noticed, the phone doesn't ring at all. Now it is very quiet. Days have passed without me leaving the house or changing out of my pyjamas. It occurs to me that my decline can be traced through the growth of the wild beard which I'm now staring at in the mirror. I never decided to grow facial hair, but there just didn't seem to be much point shaving without work to go to. Instead, I've allowed rogue grey strands to sprout in abundance at angry angles from the area around my mouth and chin. The dense growth gives me the appearance of a badly groomed cave dweller; the ragged, curling wiry hair is like the bristles on a worn toothbrush. I think about what Debs said about it getting 'a bit wild', but the thought of going out to the barber shop is too daunting for today. I decide that for now I'll allow the beard to grow a little bit more.

Then I climb the stairs and begin to search through the pockets of coats and jackets until I find what I'm looking for – an old, crumpled box of cigarettes. The secret pleasure of a sneaky smoke with my morning coffee has been in my mind since I woke this morning. First, it was just a vague idea but it soon became an obsession that I knew I wouldn't be able to shake until it was satisfied. I open the packet and wince, as I see most of the thin white sticks are bent or broken, the stringy brown tobacco spilling out like the stuffing from a ripped teddy. I find one which is almost straight and work it back into shape with my fingers. I look in the same pocket for the lighter, but it's not there. I go downstairs and search on the mantelpiece above the open fire and then in the cupboard in the hall but still can't find a light.

I head into the kitchen, the cigarette dangling between my fingers. I begin looking around in growing frustration, opening drawers and checking shelves. Then I see the toaster and nod as I devise my plan. Without inserting any bread, I push down the metal lever which makes the thin red bars inside the toaster glow. I wait a couple of seconds, allowing it to heat up. I'm still a little grumpy about what my wife said to me as she left. *Will you be ok on your own?*

I'm mumbling, 'I'm a grown man... I know how to look after myself... she thinks I can't do anything.'

Then I put the cigarette in my mouth and lean over the toaster. At first, I'm not close enough because the stick is not touching the red bars, so I force myself lower. Then I see the smoke beginning to rise and my nose is filled with a bitter, burning smell. I stand up and try and take a long draw on the cigarette. But nothing happens. I hold the cigarette up but it's still not lit. I'm momentarily confused because I saw the smoke, I smelt the flame. Then ...

'Holy fuck, my beard!'

Now I'm at the sink, slapping handfuls of cold water onto my face. There's a soft sizzling sound as the liquid splashes about me and some singed white hairs are on the tips of my fingers. I rush back to the mirror to inspect the damage. The beard looks terrible, although arguably not much worse than before, perhaps half an inch shorter in some parts. It's the smell that is bothering me, an acrid smokiness which seems to be inside my head, clinging to the hairs in my nostrils.

I head for the bathroom and spend some minutes in front of the mirror, waving a pair of nail scissors in the general direction of my facial hair before I give it up as pointless. Then I jump into the shower in an attempt to wash the smell away, rushing so much that I forget to place the bathroom mat on the floor outside the cubicle. When I finish and set my wet foot on the floor outside the shower, it immediately begins to slide like the arse of a duck along the surface of an icy lake. I grab for anything to break my fall, pulling desperately at the handle of the shower door.

As I plummet, the glass door comes off its rails and lands heavily on top of me and I thud onto the ground, my body still inside the shower cubicle, with my legs flailing outside. There's pain all over, where my head bounced off the shower floor; I've a twisted ankle and feel a strain in my back. I've also landed on top of a bottle of shampoo which has splashed all over my backside. As I lie there, I notice I can still smell smoke off my beard.

I struggle to lift the heavy door off my body and then limp, still naked, into the bedroom. My ankle is throbbing and the pain in my back means I'm having difficulty standing upright. I collapse onto the top of the bed, weary and full of self-pity. I've no strength left to move so I soon drift off into a troubled sleep. I dream about fire, a blaze in a forest where I'm trapped with no hope of escape – I go to scream for help but no words come. I keep trying to call for help but I can't find my voice.

I wake with a start, confused, cold and trembling. I'm not sure how long I've been asleep and I feel more tired now than before. The pains in my body have dulled but my mind is alert with the possibility of danger. I sit upright – I'm sure I heard a noise. I look around, rubbing my eyes and pondering the possibility that there's someone else in the room. I can't see anyone but I hear the noise again, then I notice some movement at the window.

The top of a ladder is resting against the windowsill outside and someone is climbing it. For a moment I'm afraid it's a burglar, until I remember that this is the day the window cleaners come. All at once I see the top of a head coming up the ladder, a mop of untidy hair, and I remember that I'm lying on top of the duvet with no clothes on. I roll quickly off the bed, towards the side furthest away from the window. I'm cowering on the ground as I hear the window cleaner clattering about and splashing water onto the glass. I peer around the corner of the bed and see the pane is covered with soapy suds. It's the best cover I'll get so I start to crawl across the floor, like a soldier in the jungle, except without clothes. I reach for the door handle and slither out into the landing. . .

Onto the landing, where there's another window. And where the other window cleaner, at the top of a second ladder, is cleaning streaks off the glass. He's staring in through the glass as I crawl along the floor. Naked. I look up, he looks in. There's nothing else to do so I wave at him and then, staying as low to the ground as I can, I continue moving, back into the bathroom. In there, I want to lock the door, to stay hidden away for the rest of the day.

Now I'm sitting on the still wet floor with my knees pulled up to my chin and my head down, overwhelmed with shame. I'm wondering if I can manage to get through the rest of my life without ever having to see the window cleaners again. The social ignominy of having dirty windows is surely preferable to this.

Then the doorbell rings. For a moment, the meaning of this doesn't trickle through. Then it does. The window cleaners want their money. Of course they do. Whatever embarrassment they may feel about the odd encounter with me does not override their desire to be paid. I remain sitting on the floor, paralysed by fear. Then the doorbell rings again, a longer and more determined push. I can't very well pretend that I'm not in – they've already seen me, that's after all the root of the problem – so I pull myself off the floor and dress hurriedly in my pyjamas. I'm considering ways of paying without having to see them face to face, perhaps dropping some coins out of the window or feeding them through the letterbox. But I don't know the exact amount and such a course of action would undoubtedly further deepen their already low opinion of me. The doorbell rings again.

I go downstairs, take a deep breath and open the door. Two middle-aged men, not much older than I am, are standing there, with cloths and buckets. I immediately make a mental note of which one was at the bedroom window and which the hallway. I try to smile.

'Alright, chaps. How much do I owe you?'

'Twelve pounds will do it, mate.'

It's the window cleaner from the bedroom window who answers. I notice the guy from the hallway window is looking away, far into the distance. I dash off to grab my wallet and thrust some notes and coins into his hand. I've no idea how much I've given him and he pockets it without checking. The bedroom window cleaner stands there, staring at me.

Then he says, 'There's a bit of a nip in the evenings now – the nights are fairly drawing in.'

For a moment I'm too stunned to respond. Good Christ, I think, he wants to have a conversation with me now! 'Aye,' I respond tortuously, 'there's been a wee touch of frost a few mornings already.'

The bedroom window cleaner nods slowly, while his colleague continues to look away. There's a silence which seems to stretch on and on. Then finally the first guy breaks it.

'Aye, well, I suppose we'll see you next time then.'

'Aye, all the best now.'

I close the door and fight off the urge to bang my head against it. I'm still standing there when I hear the digital chime of my phone. I look around, running from room to room, trying to locate where the noise is coming from. I have to go back upstairs and into the bedroom. I lift the phone off the bedside cabinet just at the moment it stops ringing. I check and see the missed call from Debs. I try to phone her back but the line is engaged. When I hang up, I notice another missed call, from when I was just trying to call her. I call her again but the same thing happens. I'm properly exasperated now so I throw the phone on the bed and go back to the bathroom – where I have to fix the shower door. The phone rings again and I hobble back into the bedroom to answer it.

'Hello? Debs?'

'Hi honey, how are you?'

'I'm grand, I'm ok.'

'Are you ok? You sound a little out of breath.'

'No, I'm fine, just tidying up around the house.'

'How's your day so far? Any excitement?'

'No, no. . . all quiet.'

'Did you get your beard trimmed?'
I pause for just a second. 'Yes, I did.'
'Did you pay the window cleaners?'
'Yes, I did that too.'
'Will you remember to pick up James?'
'Yes, I'll get him.'
'I've got a couple more wee jobs I need done in town. Do you think you'll be ok to do them?'
The tone of offended impatience returns to my voice. 'Yes, yes, of course, I'll be fine. . .'

Fifteen

Bad Day, Good Day . . .

April 2017

I'm on my knees. Down on the ground in my son's bedroom surrounded by toys, scattered like so much flotsam and jetsam bobbing in the sea. It's a suitable image because I feel like a shipwreck survivor today. Exhausted, weary and on the verge of giving up. I'm having a bad day. I'm here with James – Debs is away at work so it's just the two of us in the house. I know I'm supposed to say that every moment with him is precious; every second spent together a golden memory – but I don't feel that way today. The truth is, there are times when I hate it.

There, I said it. The thing that no parent should ever even think, let alone write down. It's nowhere near lunchtime and already I've been a pirate, a monster, a cowboy, a human trampoline and a punching bag. Now a three-year-old James is pulling boxes of toys out from under his bed and emptying them on the carpet, asking me to find some trivial item not seen or bothered about in months. I scarcely know what I'm looking for as I move my hands through the piles of endless plastic junk. It's like searching for a single blade of hay in a giant pile of needles.

'Where is it, Daddy? Where is it?' he chants, his impatience rising.

It's relentless today. His voice is like a stab of pain to my head. It's as if he's attached to me, taking my energy, taking my ideas, taking my life, sucking the marrow out of my bones. If I could just have a minute to myself. Just a minute to myself. There's a molten mixture of potentially volcanic issues at play here. From my battles with my own mind, my lack of self-confidence and low mood, to my son's constant need for attention and his rampant, inexhaustible curiosity and creativity. Add into all this my feelings of guilt that I'm not enjoying this morning with him or giving him the best of me, and my worries about the lack of direction in my life since I gave up work. Yes, it's a very bad day.

I've achieved nothing yet. The breakfast dishes are not tidied away, the clothes not ironed. We're still in our pyjamas and I haven't written a word or had a productive thought – any thoughts I've had recently about doing some freelance journalistic work or even doing some of my own writing will have to be put firmly aside for today. The sense of waste is upon me. Wasted time, wasted potential. I've been trying to get into the shower for more than an hour. Jesus, if I could just get a minute to myself. I think about all the things I have to do, and it all threatens to overwhelm me, to drown me. I feel the familiar line of cold sweat on my spine and know that a panic attack is sweeping across me like a sandstorm. I feel the anxiety spreading in my stomach and chest like a weed. There is no joy in parenting when I feel like this.

I go into the toilet and lock the door, hoping it will pass. But James is knocking within seconds.

'Come and play, Daddy. Come and play!'

I want to put my head on the floor, my cheek against the cold tiles and shout, *Enough! Enough! Enough! Please just leave me alone!* Instead, I open the door and he has me by the arm, leading me downstairs, explaining some new game he has invented and my role in it. We sit together on the carpet in the front room, and he starts to wheel a toy car around me. I feel like I'm going to burst into tears. I feel it is all falling apart again.

I decide we have to get out of the house. I'm claustrophobic in here, like I'm about to burst out of my own skin. I tell him that we'll go to the park. It has been a fine and sunny morning – at least we can run around, get some fresh air. I put on his clothes and shoes and open the front door. At that exact moment, it starts to rain. Not gradual, the way rain usually comes in this part of the world, but sudden and immediate and heavy. It's an angry rain, the fat drops pounding the tarmac of the road and then bouncing up again. We don't even make it past the doorstep before we have to retreat back inside. It's a really, really bad day.

We go into the front room. I put something on the TV, some cartoon to distract him for just a few minutes. I sneak out and into the kitchen and sit at the table, digging my fingernails into my palms. I can hear him laughing in the next room and he sounds like a stranger. Now I'm angry with myself for neglecting him, for dumping him in front of the TV rather than trying to be a proper parent; for leaving him sitting on his own, for preferring my own company. I feel that I'm failing at this – probably the only really important thing I'll ever do in my life. Soon my son comes into the kitchen, an uncertain look on his face, holding a pale hand out towards me.

'What are you doing, Daddy?'

'Nothing, son, I'm just sitting here for a wee minute.'

'Come and sit with me, Daddy, we can watch TV.'

I summon every part of strength that I have to push the feelings of inadequacy and desolation away, back down inside my gut, and I force a smile. I can never let him see that there's anything wrong with me, never give him any reason to be anything other than utterly confident that he is surrounded by love at all times. This is my fuck-up, not his, and I have to guard him from it, always. I take his hand in mine.

'Of course, I'll sit with you, buddy.'

He leads me into the other room and sits on my knee as he follows the plot of some cartoon, turning occasionally to me to ensure that I'm paying attention. Around this time Debs unexpectedly arrives home, having finished early at work. I don't need to say anything to her; she takes one look at me and knows I'm struggling. She suggests we all take a break. We go out for a coffee and a juice and then for a short drive. We chat, about nothing in particular, but with enough mutual respect and humour that the clouds soon begin to dissolve and I remember that I am somebody after all. Just the process of having a little bit of family time, with all of us together out of the house, brings me back to a place where I'm comfortable. It's often the little things we give no thought to that have the most hold over our feelings.

As we drive through the countryside in the rain, I notice my son is getting quieter in the back. Soon he is dozing and we head for home. I lift him tenderly from the car-seat and lay him on our sofa. He sits up and looks at me with confusion for a second before he settles again on his side. His little eyes are not quite shut, as if he is asleep and awake at the same time. A tiny hand is at the side of his face. He is oblivious to his power to pull me this way and that.

I sit beside him on the sofa and read. I want my face to be the first thing he sees when he wakes up, so he doesn't have a single moment of fear or uncertainty. Then we can do whatever he wants. We can run around, play, watch cartoons, whatever he wants. Yes, it's been a bad day. So far. I suppose we all have our own versions of that. But there's one thing about a bad day. It can always get better.

***

A week or so later, and the sun is shining. It's early morning, and James is pulling out all his toys and throwing them on the ground. Again. But what caused me despair last week just seems comical today. For no reason I can begin to explain, things are all a bit brighter.

Dressing becomes a joke. I tuck his trousers into his socks and his T-shirt into his pants, just to see the look on Debs' face. Washing becomes a game, where I'm the giant towel monster chasing him around the bed. I go into the kitchen and move to give my wife a kiss, only to discover that at that exact moment she's stuffing a slice of buttered toast into her mouth. The house is full of giggles today. My son's laughter is contagious and I don't want a cure.

I'm juggling tasks better. While I play games with James, I'm also making a stock from the chicken carcass left over from last night's dinner. There's something calming in the process and I'm enjoying the tasks of reducing, tasting, seasoning and straining until I have a pure golden liquid which will be the basis of tonight's dinner. My boy and Debs have to go to the dentist in Newcastle, a small town which is about a 30-minute drive away. It could be tricky, but we sell it to James as a day out in the seaside town and he comes along happily. The one sticky moment, when he doesn't want to leave the house, is neutralised by my crazy stair dance which makes him yelp with amusement and delight.

As I drive along the coast, I watch the light breeze play with the fingers of the trees. There's a tune going round and round in my head. I realise it's Waylon Jennings' theme from the *Dukes of Hazzard*. Without even noticing, I've changed the lyrics from, 'Just the good ol' boys' to, 'Just a daddy's boy.' We're in and out of the dentist's surgery in minutes; our son emerges beaming from the building with a new sticker and the glow of congratulation. It's quite a contrast to my own dental visits, which can run long into the afternoon as a scaffold is constructed around my mouth, and never involve the presentation of a sticker.

Then we go to the play park at the seafront. It's the swings first (it's always the swings first), before Superman rescues me from disaster half a dozen times. There's a slide which scares my son a little, so he asks to sit on my knee for the first time. As we're halfway down I notice there's a puddle at the bottom of the chute. I splash through it before ending up in a crumpled heap on the ground. The backside of my jeans is now soaked, but it's ok because James is laughing again.

Then we join Debs again in a cafe for some food. It's a bit late for breakfast but I think, to hell with it, and order a full Ulster fry, complete with soda and fadge. My son sits beside me, happily eating a sausage and licking the butter off his toast. I feel warmth coming through the window, onto my face. It's still a sunny day.

Why is today so much different than the day last week? I suppose if I knew the answer to that, I wouldn't be a penniless writer. The truth is that the two days were probably not that dissimilar, aside from a degree of altered focus on my part. The day last week wasn't that bad and today wasn't that good, but maybe there are times when our minds are not equipped to deal with too many shades of grey and instead serve us up with ready-made disasters and triumphs.

I start to think that there's something maddening in how random it all is. How we're thrown up and down like some discarded plastic bottle in a rough sea. Then I stop myself. We're having a good time. Maybe it's enough for today just to leave it at that. I ask my son if he wants to go for a walk on the beach. After all, that's what you do on a sunny day.

Sixteen

The Boys' Day

June 2017

It's not like I haven't looked after my son by myself before. Since I gave up work I do it on most days – but never for the whole afternoon, evening and night with my wife gone. We've been on the trapeze before but this is the first time the safety net has been properly removed and all three of us sense the danger. There are a few nervous glances exchanged and lots of attempts to find conviction as we tell each other that it'll be fine. As my wife packs her bag for the girls' night away, James comes into the room smiling and announces that he'll 'look after daddy'. This is almost enough to snap her resolve and I have to persuade her to keep packing, reassuring her again and again that there's nothing to worry about.

My son and I wave her off shortly after lunchtime and have a few tetchy exchanges as we try to establish who's in charge, who's next in the line of authority. I can already feel time starting to slow down so I suggest we go out. I know the secret is to keep the day filled with activities, not to let boredom or resentment creep in. I fasten James into his seat in the back of my car and drive to a diner which I know he likes. It's one of those places where the waiters all wear bright red uniforms, the sound system keeps playing Everly Brothers and Buddy Holly songs and where they serve pizzas as big as car tyres. A waiter with intense, staring eyes shows us to a good table and patiently explains to me how to work the Wi-Fi. I get some cartoons on my phone for James to watch, and I begin to examine the oversized menus. He never takes his eyes off the phone as I go through the options.

'What would you like, buddy?'

'Chicken nuggets and chips.'

'Ok, well hang on, let's have a look first. Hey, they do spaghetti Bolognese. You like spaghetti, don't you?'

'Chicken nuggets and chips.'

'Or what about pizza? They do kiddie pizzas here.'

'Chicken nuggets and chips.'

'Or lasagne? Do you want to try that for a change?'

'Chicken nuggets and chips.'

'Well, how about sausages and mash? You love sausages.'

'Chicken nuggets and chips.'

I think about it, scratching my chin, as I look up and down the menu. James is still watching my phone with deep concentration.

'Ok, buddy, well I'll tell you what, you can have chicken nuggets and chips this time, just for a treat. But it's because I decided to let you have them, do you understand?'

He doesn't answer or look at me. The waiter with the staring eyes arrives and I order my son's food and a burger for myself. I expect this to be a short conversation but the waiter keeps pointing out other things on the menu, giving me further options. His gaze is fierce upon me and soon I find I've ordered an array of side dishes that I know I'll never be able to eat, just to get him to go away again.

The dishes arrive disturbingly quickly and I sort out James first, cutting up the nuggets and placing his plate close enough that he can eat without having to remove his eyes from the phone. He begins to mechanically dip thin chips in ketchup and place them in his mouth without looking. I sit back and survey my mountain of food. I'm feeling good; I feel like I've got things under control.

I take a large bite of my burger and hear and feel a sickening crack as my teeth hit something hard. I splutter the food back out again and a sizeable chunk of tooth falls into my napkin. My tongue frantically feels for the damage and finds a hole which feels about the size of Greenland. I rush to the toilet and discover one of my front teeth has snapped in half, leaving me looking like a sober Shane MacGowan. I return to the table where my son is still eating chips and watching my phone. It occurs to me that he hasn't even noticed I've been gone. The rest of the meal passes but I've lost my appetite. James has some ice cream and uses his straw to blow bubbles in a cup of juice, while I sip on coffee and think about the dentist as my tongue tries to familiarise itself with the new dental geography.

When it's time to pay, I look around to see if I can find a different waiter but the staring eyes guy catches my gaze and is over within seconds. He tells me that if I download the restaurant app on my phone then my son's meal will only cost one pound. It does seem like a decent deal and anyway, I feel powerless to resist now, so I concur. The waiter stands there smiling at me, and staring. Eventually I have to tell him.

'Well, actually I don't know how to download an app. Sorry.'

His eyes don't leave me but I think, just for a second, I see a flicker of something there.

'Would you like me to do it for you, Sir?'

I meekly agree and he takes my phone and hits a few buttons before handing it back to me.

'That's you all set up, Sir. Now you'll get notification of all our special offers and themed evenings also.'

'That's great news,' I respond weakly.

Downloading the app has saved me five pounds on the price of the meal. When I try to pay the waiter hands me the card reader and the first question it asks is do I want to leave a gratuity. I glance up and he's still smiling, eyes locked on me. My fingers hover over the little keys. The overall bill is less than twenty pounds. I can feel his gaze burning into me. I leave a tip of five pounds. The waiter asks me my plans for the rest of the day and I lie, telling him that we don't have any, just in case he decides he wants to join us.

Our next stop on our day of fun is the play park. James loves it there and it's a good way to tire him out before bed. As I park the car and start to walk down the hill towards the play area, I notice it is substantially warmer than when we left the house. The clouds have broken into thin wisps and the sun is bringing out the different shades of green and yellow in the grass. While the summer warmth is welcome, it also has the effect of making me feel uncomfortable in my clothes. I've dressed for a colder day and now I feel hot and sticky. In addition, I've been putting on weight since I stopped working in the office, my waist expanding like boiling milk in a saucepan.

My jeans were already a tight fit but the extra heat seems to have made them contract even further. This is significant because going to the park with my son is very much an interactive experience: I know I'll be moving about a lot. I'm constantly envious of the other parents who are able to sit on the bench, chatting happily and enjoying the weather, while their children amuse themselves. It's not that way with James. If he is going down the slide, then I have to go down the slide. If he is at the top of the climbing frame, then I have to be up there too. If he is playing on the pirate ship, then I'm usually Red Beard and have to stomp around pretending I've got a wooden leg and shouting, 'Wooaaaar, me hearties!' while other parents look on, bemused.

First of all, James walks towards the swings designed for small children, the ones where the seats have a protective cage. But I'm keen for him to try the 'big boy' swings, so I can feel some sense of achievement from the day. I nudge him in that direction and lift him onto one of the black plastic seats. But he's afraid and refuses to let go of my arms.

'Daddy, I don't like it – I'm going to fall off.'

I bend over until my face is at the same level as his and talk gently. I sense this is one of those significant parenting moments. 'Son, I'm going to be right here with you and no matter what happens, I'm not going to let you fall off that seat.'

He gives me a little smile of love and lets go of my arm. I give him one small push. He falls off the seat. As he gathers himself together, his face now covered in sand, he gives me a bitter look which seems to say, 'I'm never going to fall for your shit again'.

By now my shirt is soaked with perspiration and my underwear feels like it has disappeared somewhere deep inside my arse. I need to sit down, but James is just getting started, panting and demanding that we play another game. I spot a place on the bench, which appears like a mirage across the park, next to a group of mummies. Desperation forces me to think of a plan.

I lift my son out of the swing and ask him if he thinks he can beat the world record for running around the grass strip which encircles the park. Never one to duck a challenge, he's immediately excited. I tell him the starting line is at the park bench. I bark, 'Ready, steady, go!', and off he goes, spluttering happily. I sit down on the bench and stretch my legs. Some of the mummies even begin to make small talk with me. For just a short moment I know what it feels like to be normal. Some minutes later my son arrives again, gasping and looking at me expectantly. I glance at my watch.

'Bad luck, son, just outside the record, you'd better have another try.'

And off he goes again. A thought enters my head that this could be considered cruel behaviour. I sit back, pleased with myself. But the second time James arrives back at the bench, he has developed his counterattack.

'Daddy, you run with me!' he demands.

'No, no,' I respond with growing alarm. 'I'm too old to run.'

I can see the tears gathering in his eyes and I know a tantrum is not far away. Some of the mummies start to shift uncomfortably.

'Please, Daddy, please run with me,' he whimpers pathetically.

The mummies are watching me, concern in their eyes. I've trapped myself. I pull my creaking joints and bones up from the bench and begin a light jog.

'Faster, Daddy, faster.'

I try to run. It feels horrible in the tight clothes and oppressive heat. I can't bend my legs effectively in my jeans, so the run is more like a robotic straight-legged waddle. I can almost hear a voice behind me yelling, 'Run, Forrest, run!' After I've done a couple of laps, I notice that as well as my son, there are two other young children following me. I start waving my arms to shoo them away but they just wave back at me, smiling. Soon other children began to join in until it becomes like the scene in the *Rocky* movie where Sylvester Stallone goes for a training run and hundreds of children follow him.

It's a sunny Saturday afternoon, the park is full and more than half the kids here seem to be chasing me. I become aware that many of the parents are now watching me. Some are amused, some confused, some bemused and some plainly horrified. I start to worry that they might see me as some sort of sinister Paedophile Pied Piper who is going to run straight out of the park and not stop until he has led all the poor unfortunate children to his cave.

I have to bring the situation to an end. I'm knackered, I'm being followed by a group of unknown children and I'm more than aware of how stupid I look. In my breathless state I consider that the best thing to do is to collapse there on the grass in a simulation of mock exhaustion. The mummies will all applaud my wit and the children will understand that the game is over and go quietly about their business. Or so I imagine.

As I go down onto the grass, my son follows without missing a step, leaping on top of me. He must see it as some kind of continuation of the wrestling games we play at home. The rest of the kids, whether innately or by decision, do exactly the same thing until I'm buried underneath a pile of laughing pre-school children. For a moment I can't get a breath and panic, considering that this is not the way I had imagined it all ending. But it gets worse. Encouraged by James, who views the dishing out of extreme violence against my body as a measure of affection, the children start to batter me. I reckon I could have taken any of them on their own but as a group they are unstoppable. One small red-haired child, still in nappies I notice, starts to kick me repeatedly in the face with his blue wellies. Someone else who I can't see is behind me, pulling at my hair. I feel teeth biting down on my shoulder and yelp uselessly in protest. One little girl in a summer dress is ripping up handfuls of grass and attempting to shove them down my throat. I scream for mercy.

The ordeal seems to go on for a long time before I hear a couple of the mummies move over and summon their kids back. The mother of the red-haired child asks him if he's alright. Dazed and beaten, I climb back to my feet. My son is there waiting, his face full of innocence and hope.

'Daddy, did we beat the world record?'

***

It's later in the evening now and I'm holding a weary arm up to protect my eyes from the sting of the weakening, watery sun which is sinking into a coppery sky. James is jumping in the back garden, playing some imaginary game known only to himself. His golden hair is plastered across his forehead like wet grass; there's an excited, exhausted flush in his face. Anyone can see he is tired. Anyone apart from my son. I've already let it go on longer than I should have. Sometimes it's hard to let go of a special day.

Picking the right moment to put him to bed is an exercise in timing, like trying to snatch a young salmon out of a fast-flowing river. Too early and he's still got energy and meets you with rage. Too late and he's overtired and meets you with rage. I think it's the latter now. I begin the process by calling out to him. He pretends not to hear. I let it go a couple of minutes and then do it again, with the same result. I move towards him.

'Come on now, buddy, time to go up.'

Still no acknowledgement – he's concentrating on two toy cars, one in each hand.

'We've had a great day, buddy, we've been to the diner and the park, but it's story time now.'

I move towards him and, although still pretending not to see me, he darts away as I get close. I entertain the game for a short time, enjoying his manic giggles as I chase him around the garden. Soon I have to lift him. He goes through the motions of roaring at me and swinging his arms but I can feel exhaustion pouring out of his limbs and I know his heart's not in it. His growls soon soften and he rests his burning cheek against me, and finally we go upstairs.

I know I should really bath him but it's late and we're both flagging. I settle instead for washing his face, hands and arms and brushing his teeth. He gets a new jolt of energy as I'm undressing him and we play fight on the bed for a few minutes. I help him with his pyjamas. I know he can do it himself and I know I should let him but there's a comfort for both of us in doing it together, fastening the small plastic buttons. As I read his book of choice, he asks where Mummy is on several occasions and I remind him that she's gone away for the night. He is not used to the bedtime routine without her. I think bitterly of how many bedtimes I missed in his short life because I was working late in the office.

He asks if he can sleep in our bed. I probably should encourage him to go to his own bed, but then he's my boy, my only child. I know it won't be too many more years before he won't even want to sit in the same room as me and will think the guy who pushes the trollies around the

Tesco carpark is cooler than his daddy. If he wants to sleep in our bed, then that's just fine.

I take off my shirt and cuddle in beside him. He puts his face against my chest. There's an unspoken intimacy in his skin against mine, a link which goes back to when he was a baby and I had to get up in the middle of the night to feed and wind him. Then he was so small that he could fit in the palm of one of my hands, and he'd rest his soft little head against my shoulder. It made me feel that I was his whole world.

Soon he is asleep, snoring softly, moving around the bed like a drunk man. I could leave him now, go downstairs to watch TV, surf the web or check in with people I don't really know on social media. Instead, I decide to stay and watch him sleep. As he murmurs quietly, I can't help but wonder what's going on in his head. What dreams and fears are trying to form which he doesn't yet understand? His pale skin is slightly illuminated by the bedside lamp and as I watch, I'm so in love. The tantrums, questions, demands, insults, slaps and the early mornings all feel gloriously inconsequential. Now, like this, with his thin chest rising and falling, I want time to stop. I want to throw something around him to protect him against the journey we all must take. I feel that I couldn't bear it if he were to ever suffer or be unhappy like me. I feel that I want to take all the pain in his life and absorb it into my own body. He turns over, his twig-like arm reaching out, as if searching for something. It comes to rest on my stomach and a little bit of the warmth of his hand transfers to me. I know I'm being selfish; I know to even think about denying anyone any aspect of their own journey is the worst sin.

People tell me a lot these days that I'm 'a good daddy'.

Good because I care so much, do so much, put so much of myself into it. But here, as the last of the evening light disappears like a snubbed candle, I don't feel that way. It's always at night when I am least certain, when the doubts affect my mind the most. I wonder if other parents get these thoughts. Perhaps I do what I do because I want to feel needed; I want to feel that he depends on me entirely. That's my comfort. I need to be part of everything that he is and does and will be. What's the hardest part of parenting? Letting go. Letting go that little bit more every time the sun rises.

He doesn't fit in the palm of my hand anymore and I don't feel like I'm his whole world now. But I'm still his daddy. Tiredness is coming on me too now and I sink down into the bed. I put an arm around him and he moves in close. I turn off the light.

We lie like that for some time. I suppose I must have dozed off, but after a while I'm aware that he's stirring beside me. It's dark now and I turn on the lamp once more. James is sitting up; he's afraid at first but his features relax when he sees me.

'I'm thirsty, Daddy.'

I give him a cup of water. He drinks for a long time but when he hands the cup back to me, I notice that he's only taken a very small amount. He moves closer beside me again.

'Daddy, are you going to stay with me?'

'Yes, son, yes I am.'

'And will you keep the light on, Daddy?'

I hesitate for a moment, I'm not sure if I should indulge this or resist. His little bottom lips trembles.

'Please, Daddy, I'm afraid of the dark.'

My resistance melts faster than the Easter snow.

'Of course, buddy, of course I'll keep it on.' Then, 'You know son, Daddy's afraid of the dark as well.'

He looks at me without comprehension. We settle down once more. Within minutes I can hear a soft contented growl and I know he's sleeping again. And we lie there just like that, protecting each other.

Seventeen

The World's Least Likely Blogger

July 2017

I walk past the door a couple of times before I gather enough courage to enter. I'm talking to myself as I join the queue. *You've every right to be here, as much right as anyone else.* I notice that the majority of the people in the queue are attractive young women, uniformly stylish and with impeccable make-up and hair. I'm overcome by a sense of the absurdity of me being among them, and I want to retreat. But before I can make a decision I'm being greeted at the door by another handsome young woman with a clipboard.

'Name?'

'Uh. . . it's Jonny. . . Jonny McCambridge.'

'And your Instagram handle?'

'Huh?' I reply impressively.

'Your Instagram handle? So we can put you on our mailing list.'

'Uh. . . I'll have to ask my wife. She looks after things like that for me.'

Then, inexplicably, I look over my shoulder, as if expecting Debs to appear behind me. The clipboard woman's black-lined eyes follow my gaze.

'Um,' I explain, running my hand through my hair, 'she's not here – she's at home.'

The young woman stares at me, her perfectly groomed eyebrows rising just a fraction. I get the strong feeling that she doesn't like me very much.

'Ok, well take a seat, we'll be starting in a minute.'

I wander into the cavernous room. It's a trendy bar which, naturally, I've never been in before. It's adorned with long pine tables, high chairs and heavy, glittering chandeliers. I search for a free seat but there are only faces, lots of faces and the buzz of enthusiastic chatter. It's no secret that I struggle in social situations like this. I stick out like a thumb that's been stretched on a torture rack.

Eventually I find a free seat beside a woman wearing a black dress with white spots and a smart hat, who looks like she might have been born in the same decade as me (although I sense this observation would not make a good conversational ice-breaker). She forces a smile as she moves her bag off the seat I'm about to sit on. We exchange some small talk and she starts to tell me about her blog. It's something to do with make-up and I'm desperately trying to think of an intelligent question to ask her about it. I can't. I wait for her to ask me a question about my blog – but she doesn't.

There's a short awkward silence before she speaks again. 'These events are great for bloggers, you can do so much networking, meet so many new people.'

I nod my head in apparent agreement, although I hold the opposite view. The reason I do blogging is because it means I don't ever have to meet new people – it's something I can do in the bedroom under the covers. I'm only here because my wife thought it would be a good idea and wanted to get me to leave the house for a change. But as the woman smiles, I nod again.

A heavily made-up woman in a stylish white dress makes her way up onto a little stage at the front of the bar and begins the event which she refers to as the 'Bloggers' Brunch'. We're all here to exchange ideas and contacts and to learn how to grow our audience. Our compère then tells us that as a special treat, a celebrity guest will be the first speaker. A glamorous younger woman wearing a sparkly top joins her on the stage. The compère says her guest needs no introduction, as she is one of Northern Ireland's 'top influencers'. I ask a man sitting near me who she is but I'm quickly shushed.

The young woman takes the microphone. I estimate that she's less than half my age, probably not long out of her teens. She coughs nervously, then begins to speak. She tells us about how many thousands of people read her blogs on her daily fitness routine, how she takes what she does very seriously, and talks about the importance for her of sending out the right message. I listen intently. She says she has to be very careful about what brands she endorses and that she has to feel very strongly about a product before she will support it. She confides that she's turned down big money offers because she just didn't feel strongly enough about a brand or product. There are nods around the room and a general hum of agreement. She suggests that we all need to think about what products we feel strongly about. I make a mental list of my own favourite products – Spam, man-size tissues, toilet duck, corned beef, HP sauce, coal.

As this 'top influencer' continues to speak, I find myself reflecting on the journey which has brought me to this point. A year ago, I was spending more than 70 hours a week in a hectic newspaper office environment, fielding dozens of communications every day, taking scores of key decisions to ensure our daily deadline was met; I was the focal point of and driving force behind the combined efforts of a very busy team of journalists. Now I spend long periods of time on a daily basis talking to no one but my young son. Before, I had to put my phone on silent some evenings just to get a break; now it seldom rings at all. I now don't regret any part of my lifestyle choice – except for the really bad days, I love being able to spend time with James, and the slower pace of life has certainly reduced my stress levels. I'm sleeping better now than I ever have; I'm definitely healthier and happier. But that doesn't mean I don't feel cut off now and then, or that I don't sometimes have a troubling sense that the world is passing me by. Perhaps I'm just a little lonely but I do feel that I need some connection with the bigger conversation; that I should sometimes be pondering weightier questions than whether to cook potato waffles or alphabet spaghetti for dinner.

As usual, Debs picked up on all of this before I'd even admitted it to myself. As a way of providing me with a diversion, she set me up with some social media accounts, encouraging me to engage with a world I'd always stubbornly resisted getting involved with. So I tried a few exploratory tweets on Twitter and a couple of Facebook posts. These networks allowed me to re-establish contact with a number of people I hadn't heard from in years, and even to make some new acquaintances. It was fun and many people seemed to enjoy what I had to say.

Then Debs suggested that I should start my own blog. I know her intention was to give me a creative outlet but for a technophobe like me it seemed like a stretch too far – and I told her so. But, as I continued to share experiences and silly gags on Facebook, more and more people kept suggesting the same thing to me: *why don't you start your own blog?* Usually, it takes a long time for my mind to adapt to a new concept, but I started to think about it. What would a blog from me look like? What would I put in it? The idea was floating somewhere in my mind one day as I lay on the sofa watching He-Man on TV with James. It was getting to a good bit, when Skeletor attacked Castle Greyskull. He (James, not Skeletor) looked at me, golden curls framing his little face, his eyes filled with an insatiable appetite for new knowledge.

'Where's Mummy, Daddy?'

'Mummy's at work, son, in the office.'

'And why don't you go to work anymore, Daddy?'

I moved awkwardly in my seat and tried to distract him away from a conversation I wasn't ready to have. 'Watch the programme, son. Look, Man-at-Arms has been turned to stone. What do you think He-Man will do about this?'

His innocent face creased with curiosity, although I sensed it was not from concern over the fate of Man-at-Arms.

'Daddy?'

'Yes, son?'

'What's a daddy for?'

The question stuck with me and when I did launch a blog, that's what I decided to call it – *What's A Daddy For?* It seemed an apposite and quirky thought with which to start a new venture. I wrote a few lighthearted tales about parenting and the unfamiliar challenges of being a stay-at-home father and posted them nervously to an unknown audience. I was surprised when after just a few hours, I had attracted hundreds of readers. The reaction was mostly positive, and within days I was fielding requests from radio stations to go into their studios to discuss topical family and social issues on air. I was generally cast as the slightly confused father muddling through day by day and making silly jokes, with a child psychology expert on the other end of the line to give calm and measured advice about how it should really be done.

Mumsnet, the popular parenting forum, soon took an interest in my writing, selecting some of my posts to be their 'Blog of the Day', which helped to drive more readers to my site. Soon I began to talk about mental health issues on the blog, and this opened up an even wider audience and started a deeper conversation. The relative novelty of a man from Northern Ireland talking about depression ensured that I received more broadcast requests. Then I was asked to do some advocacy work for mental health charities and to contribute magazine articles or posts for other, third-party blogs on the subject. When a couple of newspapers wrote stories about my experiences including how I'd had to walk away from that very industry, I was aware there was a certain irony at work.

The popularity of the blog grew steadily and within just a few months I'd gathered a small but significant following. I found there was no shortage of people prepared to give me information on what I had to do to grow my audience; how I needed to become part of the blogging community; how I had to think about monetising my site; how I could go about creating a 'sticky' blog. Soon PR companies began to get in touch, asking if I'd promote events they were involved with or if I'd try out products they were supporting. I actually made one single, ill-advised foray into the world of commercial blogging which ended in ignominy and with my fee being left unpaid, after I'd composed a post poking fun at all the rules and preconditions the company I was working with had ordered me to comply with when putting blogs together for them.

The blogging community, as I quickly discovered, is vast. The easy accessibility of the form is both its strength and weakness. Soon, as part of a huge blogging network, I was able to access hundreds of posts every day from aspiring writers. The democracy of countless writers sharing their thoughts on every possible subject at any time can certainly be stimulating. But the lack of any quality control was stark – finding a proper writer or a distinctive voice among the sludge was like searching for a diamond ring in a sewer. More often than not, an obsession with the size of the audience of a platform trumped proper care for the craft. And as someone who had learned how to write the long, hard way – through the daily graft of a working journalist – and who had a love of and respect for words, I quickly grew frustrated with this.

***

By now a procession of people, almost all young women, have been up on the stage, each one determined to make the most of the allotted two minutes to present their blog. Most have talked about networking, or how to grow an audience, or the importance of 'selling yourself' if you want to stand out from the crowd. And there's been an awful lot of talk about fashion and make-up.

The compère climbs back onto the stage, flushed with the contagious excitement of the event. She begins to speak: 'Well, we've had a great day. I think almost everyone has had the chance to say something. One of the best things about the blogging community in Belfast is how we're like a big family. We all know each other's names. Now, is there anyone else who hasn't spoken?'

I find myself walking slowly to the stage. The compère studies me.

'I'm sorry,' she says, 'but I don't know your name.'

I take the microphone.

'That's alright. I'm Jonny.' I scratch my chin and think about what to say. 'Well, I run the blog, *What's a Daddy For?* It's small and I only started a few months ago, so you might not have heard of it. On it I talk a bit about being a dad, and a bit about struggling through the mental health problems which caused me to leave my job. . . '

There's a murmur from the crowd. I hesitate before going on.

'I'm not really sure why I'm here. I don't really do well with meeting people. I don't do networking; I don't do any product placement; and I don't much care how many people read my stuff. I've never made a penny from my blog and I don't suppose I ever will. I guess I'm the world's least likely blogger! But the reason I do it is because I like to tell stories. If I have anything to say today, then it's to remember to take care over the art of telling the story.'

There's more confused murmuring as I leave the stage.

Next, the compère encourages us to chat with each other informally. As new friendships are being formed, I quickly head for the door. But barring my way is the young woman with the clipboard who greeted me on my arrival here – the one who I sensed didn't like me very much.

'You're not leaving already? This is where we all do the networking bit and get to know each other – it's a lot of fun.'

'I know but I really have to get home. I've already stayed longer than I intended to.'

'But we'll be giving out make-up samples soon.'

'Uh. . . I really need to be going.'

I'm already halfway through the door when she speaks again.

'Well, will you come again? I thought it was so refreshing what you said up there. Also, I think your blog is fantastic. I love reading your stories, Jonny. Please come to the next brunch.'

I stop for just a moment.

'OK then, maybe I will.'

Eighteen

My Wife's on the Telly

August 2017

I'm in the fruit and veg section of the corner shop, holding an avocado in each hand. I'm squeezing each one gently, shaking my head and mumbling words of displeasure. James is snapping impatiently at my ankles.

'Can I have a packet of crisps, Daddy?'

'In a minute, son, I'm trying to work out what to make for dinner. We need to get something nice for Mummy coming home from work.'

I notice two women coming towards me. I recognise them as staff who work on the tills here. My first thought is that they may be about to complain about me getting too tactile with the produce, and I slyly hide my hands behind my back. Instead, they stand in front of me, smiling expectantly.

'Hey, Mister. . .' the shorter one begins. 'Hey, Mister.'

'Uh-huh?'

'Your wife's on the telly. I've seen her doing the news.'

She seems to be telling me, rather than asking me, so I just nod along. I don't need to respond anyway because she keeps talking.

'Aye, I've seen her on loads of times. The first couple of times I couldn't think who she was – I just knew the face. And then it hit me, that's the wee girl that comes into our shop to buy magazines. So, I was watching the news last night, and I said to my Ma, "Ma, that wee girl on the news comes into our shop sometimes to buy magazines." And my Ma says, "Are you sure that's the same girl?" and I says, "That's definitely the wee girl that comes into our shop and she's really nice – she's just like a normal person." And my Ma says, "It just goes to show, you just never know who you're going to meet in the shop, so you don't."'

The taller woman with the glasses is nodding along enthusiastically. And they both smile at me. I decide I'll have to say something in response.

'Yes, well, she's doing very well – and this wee man is very proud of his mummy.'

I'm about to ruffle James' hair before I remember I'm holding an avocado. The shorter woman wants to keep the conversation going.

'I don't know how she does it, standing there live on the telly with a microphone. I think I'd shite myself if I had to do that.'

The taller woman nods quickly in agreement.

'Well, I'd better go,' I mumble, 'I promised James I'd get him a packet of crisps.'

Before I can get away, the shorter woman places a hand on my arm.

'And what do you do, Mister? Do you work on the TV too?'

'No, no, uh. . . I just do bits and pieces. . . and I look after our son.'

She takes a step back. I think I see a quick flash of pity in her eyes.

'Well, when you see your wife, can you tell her that we said hello? And tell her that we think she's great on the telly.'

'Yes, I'll certainly do that.'

I wander off towards the meat counter, James skipping just behind me.

'Shall I make spaghetti Bolognese tonight, son?'

'Can I have crisps instead, Daddy?'

A few minutes later we're walking home; I'm checking my phone while James is eating his crisps. I notice a missed call from a number I don't recognise. I check my messages and there's a voicemail from a male caller, telling me he works as a producer on a local radio show and wants me to go on air tonight. He asks if I can call him back as soon as possible. As I mentioned, because of my work on the blog, I sometimes get asked to go on the radio – usually to discuss some parenting issue, as part of a filler segment in the gap between news bulletins. I generally try to help out if I can.

I call the number back and the producer answers on the second ring.

'Hi, you were looking for me?' I begin.

'Jonny, is that you? Thanks so much for getting back to me.'

'That's fine.'

'You see Jonny, the thing is, we were hoping you might be able to come into the studio tonight. We're all big fans of your blog in here – we think it's hilarious, all those stories about what you get up to with your son. It's brilliant, what you're doing.'

The man is young and enthusiastic, trying too hard to make a good impression. He talks to me as if I'm an old friend, although I'm fairly sure I've never spoken to him before now.

'Well, um . . . what is it you want me to talk about?'

'Right, Jonny, there's been this story in the news today. It's about this bishop – the angle is that she's a woman, and she's spoken out about how difficult it is for her to get acceptance in a male-dominated profession. She says she usually gets mistaken for the bishop's wife or even his secretary. And we thought it would be great to have you in to have a chat about it.'

'Right, um, okay. It's an interesting story but I don't really know what angle I could bring to it. Wouldn't it be better to have a female voice on this?'

There's a short silence before he goes on.

'Well, you know, Jonny. . . She's a woman in a man's world – and you know. . . you're a man in a woman's world. I think it would make for a really interesting perspective, the things you have to put up with. You must hear all sorts.'

I'm a little bit surprised and stung. I tell him that I'm busy later on and once he realises I'm not interested, he changes his tone and cuts the conversation short. I put the phone back in my pocket and walk a few steps further before James slides a warm little hand inside mine.

'Who was that on the phone, Daddy?'

'That was just work, buddy, nothing important.'

'Do you have to go away to work tonight?'

'No, no, I'm not going anywhere.'

Soon we're home again and I'm slicing onions and browning some mince in a heavy iron pan while James plays a game on my phone and munches his crisps. But I keep forgetting what I'm supposed to be doing, my mind slipping back to the two conversations from earlier. The women in the shop who recognised my wife from the TV, and the radio producer who said I was a man living in a woman's world. As I clean my son's hands, I can't stop the feeling from creeping over me that I'm missing out on something; that the big journey is continuing without me.

When Debs and I first got together, we were both

young and ambitious journalists. In our marriage we've always tried to approach every situation as a team, making decisions and financial commitments together. But because I was a few years older, I had been in the trade a bit longer and, consequently, had risen a little higher in the ranks. And although I would never have said it out loud, the fact that I earned more money than Debs undoubtedly fit the very traditional familial template for the sexes ingrained in my psyche. While mouthing all the right words about equality, I suppose I quietly felt that I had achieved what was expected of the male partner. When James was born, Debs was the one who made sacrifices in her career to care for his needs while I expected to continue my inevitable rise in the profession.

Then of course everything changed. After I left my job, it seemed logical that I would take on the bulk of the daily childcare responsibilities. And while I threw myself into a routine of nursery and then school runs, play dates and birthday parties, Debs' career quickly progressed. When she took a job as a broadcast journalist for a local TV station, her profile soared. Northern Ireland is a small place, and there have been frequent conversations of the sort I had in the shop earlier. I'm desperately proud of what my wife has achieved and never tire of answering questions about her. I don't mind at all being the guy who's married to the girl off the telly.

However, none of this was planned. My decision to leave work was made swiftly and out of necessity, for health reasons – it wasn't really a choice. The other consequences only emerged later – the fact that I'm no longer the main breadwinner and now spend most of each day with my son. I've had to adjust to a life without the goal of career advancement. And, inevitably, there are times when I ask myself: is it enough?

I've been teased on nights out with male friends about living off my wife and have had a few awkward conversations with the other dads at the school gates when they ask if, like them, I'm working the night shift. But there's no point in trying to externalise this as a problem for other people. The truth is nobody cares what I'm doing with my life; whether I'm working or not. Nobody but me.

I was a little bit irked by the clumsy approach of the young radio producer today. It's easy to think that it was an annoyance on my part at the outdated perceptions other people can have about traditional gender roles. But the real truth might be that I bristled because it was a little bit too close to what's going on in my own head. Buried somewhere deep down, is there a small part of me which is ashamed of being the one standing at the school gates? Is there a pathetic part of my mind that still insists that because I'm the man, I should be doing more; that is embarrassed at the weakness which my mental collapse exposed?

James moves beside me, puts a hand on my leg.

'Daddy, are you crying?'

I quickly wipe the corners of my stinging eyes on my sleeve.

'No, son, it's these bloody onions. They're cutting the eyes out of me.'

'What are we going to do tonight, Daddy?'

'Well, first you can go for a ride on your bike. Then we can watch Mummy on the TV, and then we'll have our dinner. How does that sound?'

'What are we having?'

'I told you, I'm making spaghetti Bolognese.'

'Can I have potato waffles instead?'

We go outside and I help him onto the small green and black bicycle. Riding the bike has come to symbolise something much more important than it should in my own journey as a parent. James was slow to embrace the bike we bought him for his birthday last year, insisting until only recently that he would never ride it, and becoming upset when I tried to encourage him towards it. I had to start by helping him overcoming his fear, persuading him that it was something to be enjoyed, not afraid of. Then slowly, taking small steps at first, we made progress. I persuaded him to sit on the saddle, then to pedal, then to allow me to let go. I kept reassuring him, gently pulling him back when he resisted my suggestions, until I felt he was beginning to have fun.

Now I'm walking alongside him, guiding him down into the cul-de-sac where I know there are no cars. His little face strains with the effort of pushing the pedals and his oversized safety helmet looks faintly absurd, like a giant eggcup which has been glued to his head. But he's enjoying the movement as he gets to the top of the hill, picking up a little speed. I'm starting to sweat and pant as I struggle to keep up.

'Can I try going down the hill now, Daddy?'

'Ok, buddy, just take it easy – not too fast.'

At this he disappears down the slope of the road, and I break into a run in an unsuccessful attempt to keep close to him, panic rising.

'Slow down, son, slow down!'

'I don't know how to, Daddy!'

'Use the brakes! The brakes!'

This proves to be spectacularly bad advice, because as soon as he applies pressure on the brake handle the front wheel locks, causing the back of the bike to first wobble and then move sideways. I'm sprinting as I watch my son crash heavily onto the hard road.

'Oh fuck! Balls! Shite!' I curse under my breath. Then, 'Are you alright, son?'

I lift the bike off him and see the first tears come. He has small cuts on both knees and a series of nasty red scrapes on one arm.

'I want Mummy! I want Mummy!'

'I know you do, buddy, but Daddy is here now.'

When we get back into the house, I cuddle him and clean his wounds, whispering encouragement in his ear. He's naturally annoyed that I can't find the colourful Mickey Mouse plasters that Debs uses, and scowls at me for some minutes. Then, when he calms down, I take him outside again and lift him back onto the bike, mindful of the importance of not letting the fear and the pain be the last feelings he remembers. He cycles on, gingerly at first, until his confidence returns and again I have to chase after him to keep up. Soon we're both flushed and exhausted.

'Alright, buddy, do you want me to give you a wee treat while we watch Mummy on TV?'

Minutes later he's cuddled into my side on the sofa as news time approaches. He's forgotten about the crash and is licking a yellow lolly while I press buttons on the remote control.

'It's channel number three, Daddy.'

'Yes, I know, I know . . . Got it now.'

There are a couple of news reports before the image of Debs fills the screen; she's standing outside a courthouse holding a microphone. James gives a little involuntary jump of excitement.

'Remember, buddy,' I begin, 'if Mummy nods her head that means she's saying, "Hello James".'

We watch a few seconds more before James leaps again.

'She did it, Daddy! I saw Mummy nod her head!'

'That's right, son, and remember if Mummy waves her arm that's her saying, "I love you James".'

Another moment.

'Yes, Daddy! Look, she waved her arm, she's doing it!'

The report finishes and I'm moving back towards the kitchen to check dinner when I receive a text message. It's from Debs: *Hi honey. Work's crazy busy tonight! Won't be back for a while. Kiss James for me. Love you both xxxx.*

I go back to the living room where James is now playing with Lego. I read the message silently one more time.

'Hi, buddy,' I begin, 'Mummy's going to be a little later tonight. So it's a Daddy-and-James night, ok?'

He looks up quickly and I know immediately that he's struggling to contain his emotions. And that he blames me for the unwelcome development. He throws a piece of Lego onto the carpet.

'Why is Mummy not home now, Daddy? I want her home!'

'I know you do, son, but something important has come up at her office. So we'll get some dinner together and then I'll run your bath and we can cuddle up together and read a wee book.'

But there are fat tears in his eyes now as he begins to knock over Lego constructions, scattering small bricks across the carpet.

'But I don't want to cuddle with you, I want Mummy to put me to bed!'

I withdraw from the room, judging that my presence is increasing his agitation, rather than soothing it. In truth I'm a little bit annoyed myself as I stir the Bolognese sauce. Annoyed that Debs is working late again and that I'm having to assume the childcare responsibilities on my own – a role that I can never walk away from. But as I stand there, stirring and stewing, a new thought comes to me. I think about the hundreds of days when I was late home from the office. How I became so obsessed with my responsibilities and didn't think enough about the people who were waiting at home for me. How I always expected a warm reception and a soft passage back into domestic existence, no matter how late I returned from work. That's what I'm thinking about now.

I taste the Bolognese sauce and decide that it needs more seasoning. And then I take some potato waffles out of the freezer.

Nineteen

Starting School

September 2017

It's the night before my son starts primary school, and almost exactly a year since I left my job at the paper for the final time. Those twelve months feel like a lifetime, in which I've given virtually all of my attention to James and experienced so many parental joys and challenges that would have had to have been outsourced if I was still in the corporate world. He and I have come to lean on each other. School will represent the end of that chapter. I'm anxious for him, but a little bit for myself as well. I know the time is coming when I'm going to have to show my face out in the world again.

The uniform is bought, the new schoolbag and pencil case too. The new shoes are brilliantly pristine and polished. Debs and I will both be there in the morning to take James to the P1 classroom, to show him where his desk is and introduce him to the teacher. Undoubtedly there'll be tears from him – and from us. I'm desperately proud of him. I'm desperately nervous and afraid as well. We're as ready as we can be. Yet something doesn't feel quite right to me. There's something about the whole process which makes me want to yell, 'Stop! It's too soon!' I suppose that's the curse, the emotional tic of the parent – this feeling of never wanting to let go; the instinct that your child is better off at home with Mummy and Daddy.

My memory inevitably strays back to when I started primary school in the 1970s – a time when there were teachers who could barely contain their lust for wielding the stick or slipper. I was lucky, in that I had enough academic ability to keep me from many of the worst excesses, but I had several classmates who were ruthlessly beaten. Looking back, I recognise now that many of them clearly suffered from learning difficulties or emotional problems. Yet no allowances were made and failure at academic tasks was met with the crudest forms of discipline. Children were simply divided into those who were smart and those who were not. Those who were not were all but abandoned. And not all of the punishments were physical. One of my clearest memories of P1 is when I was punished for some supposed misdemeanour by being made to stand in the corner. I told the teacher I needed the toilet but she grimly refused to let me move. I stood there in pain for so long that eventually I wet myself, in front of the whole class. A crueller way to treat a scared four-year-old would be difficult to imagine.

But it's scarcely relevant to go over all this old stuff; the world's a very different place now. Yet the uneasiness remains. I've got my son with me now. I've been trying to keep a feeling of normality about the week while also explaining that things are about to become a bit different. And that's just it. It will all be a bit different from now on. All the time I've got with him from now on will always be before or after school, between terms or at weekends. The sense that it's just me and him and Debs, with nobody else to interfere, will never quite exist in the same way again. The bond between the three of us that's been there since his birth will inevitably loosen just a little. It will never be just us again.

And it's the first step for James on that relentless path of life – from school to university to employment. The first inching turn of the groaning, grinding old wooden wheel. The same relentless journey which almost destroyed me. And yet it has to be. I can't rewrite the world and I've got no better ideas on how else it could be done. He'll make new friends, learn how to live independently of us. It's the beginning of the biggest voyage of all. So why am I wasting my time worrying? Maybe just because I feel a sense of poignancy that I can't shift. Or maybe this is just my typically long-winded way of saying I'm going to miss my son. I know it's only for a few hours every day, but I know I'm going to miss him so much. He's so happy sitting here beside me now that it feels like it should last forever. It can't. But for now, I'm going to keep holding onto his hand for just a little bit longer.

Early the next morning, I wake and look out the window. There's no sky today, just a creamy grey void without definition where it should be. The rain's coming down, as steady as a prison sentence. James and Debs were awake before me and are already about their business. I move to the stairs and see him coming up to find me. We meet in the middle – 'like the Grand Old Duke of York', I tell him. We sit there on the stairs. He's on my knee and I'm holding him in my arms, neither of us speaking. We sit there.

I don't think any of us slept very well last night. James ended up in our bed again, stretched out horizontally like a barrier between me and Debs. Feet at her side, head at mine. I had dreams of being late on the first day. A friend had told me that the school gate closes at precisely on the minute, and if you don't make it you have to go in through the front door, past the Principal's office, to be marked as late. This is the dream I had last night – except it's me who's late, not my son.

We move from the stairs at last. I make the breakfast, cereal and a smoothie. I go to feed James but he takes the spoon and sends me away, slightly chastised. He eats everything. I can tell he's a little afraid but he wants me to know he's being brave. I ask him if he's nervous and he gives the smallest nod I've seen. I hold his hand and we watch some TV. I ask him if he wants me to dress him but he asks for his mummy – that primal bond is just a little deeper. The first tears come as the blue jumper is pulled over his head. The tiny grey shorts with a fierce crease are pulled up. He's mumbling something soft and I have to strain to hear.

'I don't want to go. I don't want to go. . .'

Debs talks to him, tells him how brave he is. How proud we are of him; how it's natural to be a little afraid on the first day. It's ok so far. Nothing worse than we expected. Just a couple of scratches, no scars. I make a small snack, facing the challenge of finding something healthy he will actually eat. I settle on a pancake and some raisins. I put the plastic lunchbox in his brightly coloured new schoolbag. There are a few more tears as we put his shoes on. But when we produce our cameras to take photos for the grandparents, a performer's smile is worn. This troubles me a little. It reminds me of my own capacity to make other people think exactly what I want them to; how I keep the real stuff packed tight inside.

The school raincoat will be needed and the schoolbag is hoisted onto his shoulders. It's so large that it seems faintly ridiculous, giving him the appearance of a snail carrying his home on his back. Of course, I have everyone in the car much too early. I'm worried about the traffic and keep thinking about being late and having to walk past the headmaster's office. But it's not that bad after all and I get parked right outside the school with time to spare. Holding both Debs' and my hands, James walks slowly through the playground, a little cowed by the presence of older and noisier children. But we see some of his friends and his face brightens a little. I know he's doing everything he can to be brave for us, and it's pulling me to bits.

The headmaster opens the front door and we move to his classroom. Every child has their own way of responding to the situation. Some rush inside, barely looking back at their tearful parents, while others need that little bit more care. Debs takes James inside and to his desk. I want to go too but decide it's better to hang back. Two parents inside seems excessive. Staying back is even harder though. My face is against the window. While Debs is with him, he's fine. Some of his friends from nursery come to play with him and I see signs of animation and excitement in his face. Some of the other parents are in the classroom too. I see one little girl who has her arm around her mother's neck, in a tight grip closer to a wrestling hold than a child's gesture of love. Soon the teacher shuts the door and Debs is gently ushered out. I can see our boy is crying now. I knew he would. But the teacher is there to comfort him and so are his friends. It's ok. There's no real distress, no sense of horror.

We retreat to a nearby coffee shop and meet with some other parents. It's almost like the aftermath of a funeral as we swap gloomy tales and anecdotes. There's some black humour amongst the tears. And then we're home again, with nothing really to do but wait until we pick him up again. Debs distracts herself with some cleaning. I write. I wonder what he's doing now. It's a funny sort of in-between time – much like the Grand Old Duke of York, we're 'neither up nor down'. But we'll find out soon enough. And that's the first morning done; one day to be chalked off the tally.

***

There's a large group of us standing behind the black steel gates. Waiting. It looks like we're part of an industrial picket outside a factory. Except that the tensions are higher here, the nerves more fraught. The school bell sounds – a nasty horn of a noise, more like a car alarm than a bell. A man with a large ring of keys opens the lock on the gates. The parents edge forward, like nervous sheep looking to be fed. The grey void of a sky is melting and a pale sun is trying to break through. There's a moment of confusion: it's the first time and nobody is really sure what happens next.

Then the teachers appear, bringing the kids out into the playground, making them stand in lines. We see James and soon we're waving furiously. He spots us and his shyness can't conceal the excited smile. The teachers let the children go one by one, once they know the right adult is there. When it's his turn, my stomach leaps. He begins to run. I hold my arms out and he runs. I kneel down and he runs. . . straight into Debs' waiting arms. She's drowning him in kisses and I have to content myself with a fatherly ruffle of his hair. But that's grand, he's back with us. The classroom assistant tells us he's been fine – there were a few tears after we left and then all calm. It's going far better than we'd hoped.

Then we take him into town in my car. We've promised him a new toy and lunch at a cafe as a treat. I fire questions at him. I want to know everything about the first day. But he's not for sharing.

'Did you play with your friends?'

He looks out the side window.

'Was the teacher nice?'

He looks out the front window.

'Did she tell you a story?'

He looks out the back window.

I feel I'm not getting the full picture. A few more of my questions are batted aside before James decides to bring a halt to the interview.

'Daddy, if you really want to know what P1 is like, then just become a kiddie again.'

I suppose we're all a bit worn out. The long build-up of emotion, the rapid release, the weary aftermath. The car is quiet now. I don't quite know what to feel. I'm thinking about a poem one of my friends reminded me of last night – 'On Children' by Kahlil Gibran. One line keeps coming to me now: 'They come through you but not from you.'

And I think this is a warning about what I'm feeling. My desire to claim my son, to own him, to stop anyone else getting a stake. But that's not the way forward. I know that he'll do better from being with all the other children, with the teacher, with all the questions. The truth is I can't stimulate him enough; there's a part of him that's outgrown me already. A part of him that needs new challenges, even if he doesn't always know it. And, even though I'm afraid, I know that's good for me too. I can't be all of him, just like he can't be all of me. I know I've been hiding behind him for many months – as a source of comfort, a good reason why I don't have to engage with society.

We're in a cafe now. James eating chips and playing with his new toy – a dinosaur set. He's babbling excitedly.

'Mummy, you can be the dinosaurs, I can be the hero.'

'Who can I be, son?' I ask.

'You can be the tree, Daddy.'

And that's it. We move on as before. He wants to go to the lake to feed the ducks next, and to jump in the puddles. It's been a busy day; a full day.

Twenty

The Drama Class

October 2017

We sit in a circle, legs crossed – my son, six other young children, and me. I'm pretending not to notice that the kids are peering at me curiously. I feel like Rodney in that old episode of *Only Fools and Horses*, when he has to pretend he's a child to get a free holiday. I feel like a plonker.

A young woman wearing a tracksuit arrives. She's thin and full of energy and childlike enthusiasm. She introduces herself as, 'Jo, the drama instructor'. As she joins us on the floor, she glances inquiringly at me and I quickly mumble an explanation. My son wants to do the class, but he's shy, and feels more comfortable if I'm in here with him. She gives a short nod which, I assume, authorises me to stay.

While Jo is explaining to the group what we're going to do in the class, I reflect upon my own acting experiences. There aren't any. Well, except for a classroom production of the assassination scene from *Julius Caesar*, when I played the crowd. It was a non-speaking role. However, my brooding intensity was much admired by my peers.

Jo starts by getting us to do a bit of superhero dancing. It's a decent warm-up. We run around in circles, each of us with a straight arm protruding, as we hum the *Superman* theme song. Any inhibitions are quickly shed. Some of these children are very vocal – I suppose this is to be expected in a drama class. They start to babble excitedly to Jo. She deals with them patiently. My wee man, on the other hand, is a little intimidated by the noise and buries his head in my chest. I tell him he doesn't have to stay – but he insists he wants to.

The theme of this week's class is monkeys. Jo tells us she wants us to act out the parts of lots of different simians. But there's a problem – I'm just not feeling it. I can't quite seem to get into character. I ask Jo what my monkey's motivation is. She answers me in the same placid, unruffled tone she uses with the kids. Then we run around the room, doing impressions of gorillas, chimpanzees, orangutans. James laughs at how animated I've become. Yet I'm aware that all of my monkey impressions are much the same – I'm worried about the apparent limitations in my range.

While I'm running around, cupping my arms and shouting, 'Ooh, ooh, ooh!', I notice that a number of adults have gathered outside and are staring in the window. But it's too late for dignity. I give them a moronic look, scratch my head and mimic eating a banana. I used to be a respected journalist, you know.

Next, Jo tells us a story. It's about lots of different types of monkeys in a zoo and is a preamble to us all acting out parts in a little sketch. My son and I are chosen to play the gorillas (a step up from being the crowd in *Julius Caesar*, I suppose), which necessitates us both beating our chests and roaring a lot. I've got an advantage here, in that this is how I usually behave when I'm about the house. Jo gives us all a couple of lines to recite. When it's our turn, I bellow them out. James whispers them. Nobody else can hear him – but I can, and that's enough. I know he's having a good time.

The class finishes with some colouring in, which I imagine is a method of calming the children down after all the monkey mayhem. Jo gives the kids a bag of sweets each and then we're off. She asks me if we'll come back next week. I tell her we will if James wants to.

The drama class is indicative of how the world has changed since I was a kid. Then education finished when the school bell rang. You sprinted out of the building, said goodbye to your chums and then spent the rest of the day coming up with useless ways to amuse yourself.

But society has a firmer grip now. Education is a much broader concept. We're continually being told that the most important learning takes place in the home. What is begun at school with the teacher should be continued by the parents.

And opportunities are everywhere now. The number of extra-curricular activities available to children today is, frankly, mind-boggling. In our boy's short life so far, he's already taken classes in swimming, tennis, yoga, taxidermy, rugby, football, music, Morris dancing, goat staring, yodelling, goose counting and navel-fluff collecting . . . Ok, I've made some of these up, but you get the idea! These days there's an obsession with making sure kids don't miss out on anything. Give them every chance. After all, they might become the next ballet genius, piano virtuoso, Wimbledon champion . . .

***

Seven days later, and my son and I are back sitting on the same floor with the same group of other children. In the interim, I'd asked James if he'd be comfortable going to drama class on his own this time. No chance! Jo arrives and gives me a little smile – whether it's encouragement or pity, I can't tell. Just like last time, she welcomes everyone to the class with a gush of girlish cheerfulness. Boy One asks her if we'll be getting a bag of sweets again this week (I'm keen to know myself, but don't like to say). Jo smiles.

We start by playing a game which is new to me – 'Duck, Duck, Goose'. For some reason I can't seem to grasp the rules and it quickly descends into farce. What happens is that Boy Two walks round the circle, tapping everybody on the head and softly saying 'duck', until he gets to me, when he wallops me painfully on the back of the skull and screams 'goose!'. I stare vacantly at him. Eventually Jo explains to me that I'm supposed to chase him. I half-heartedly comply. Then I sit down again. Boy Two calls me a 'dimwit'. Jo tells him that's not very nice and asks him to apologise. He glowers at me. Jo smiles.

Next, Boy Three walks around the circle, tapping everyone on the head and quietly saying 'duck'. When he reaches me, he whacks me painfully and bellows 'goose!' right into my ear. I chase him around but it's not clear what I'm meant to do if I catch him. I assume tripping him up is forbidden. Jo persists with the game for a while, but abandons it when it becomes clear the children are simply using it as an excuse to hit me really hard on the head. One of my ears is ringing slightly.

Boy One asks once again if we're getting a bag of sweets this week. Jo smiles. Then she gathers us in a circle and asks us to guess what's in her bag. Boy Two suggests that it might be poo. Jo smiles. It's not poo, it transpires – it's a toy rattlesnake called Rex. We're each encouraged to touch Rex, as if he were a real snake. Boy Three asks if he can see Rex's guts. Jo smiles. Then, when Boy Two is holding Rex, he tells her that a frog once pissed on his mummy's hand. When Jo expresses scepticism, Boy Two tells her that his mummy then licked the pee. Boy One tells Jo that his mummy eats dog poo. Jo smiles.

Undaunted, she starts to tell us a story about Rex. It involves him not being very good at dancing (no arms and legs, you see). I've got empathy and nod sadly – but Jo seems to have lost the rest of the room. Boy Three is lying stretched out on the floor, making farting noises. Boy One has moved behind Jo and has picked up her mobile phone. He is pressing keys maniacally. I decide I'd better warn her and she jumps upright in alarm. She tells Boy One that he's not allowed to be 'invasive'. He sits down and gives me a wretched look, which seems to be his way of telling me he'll get me later for grassing him up.

Boy One then asks if we're getting a bag of sweets this week. Jo smiles. She says it's time now for us to act out a short sketch. I happily volunteer to be a dancing penguin. It just feels right. But everybody else wants to be a snake. She asks Boy Three to be a swan, to which he roars back, 'I hate bloody swans!' So Jo decides he can be a snake. While we're acting out the sketch, Boy One is up to his old tricks, rifling through Jo's handbag. I decide to let it go this time.

I execute an admirable solo number as a tap-dancing penguin, but it can't save the sinking ship. Boy Two is supposed to be a bear. He's lying flat under the table, apparently asleep. When Jo asks him why he's not dancing, he says the bear is dead. Our sketch concludes. Jo smiles.

It's time for colouring in – fittingly, a picture of a snake. I give it my best but Boy Three tells me my picture looks like 'poopy pants'. I'm a little hurt, but I can sort of see where he's coming from. Jo takes the sweets from her bag and starts to distribute them. But this week it's individual sweets rather than packets, and Boys One, Two and Three protest angrily. I'm carried along by the raw emotion and have to stop myself from yelling, 'I only came for the fecking sweets!' Jo ends up giving Boys One, Two and Three another sweet, but the tension in the room is unmistakeable. Jo smiles weakly.

Finally, it's time to gather our belongings. Jo is handing a schoolbag to Boy Two, when it becomes clear he's about to sneeze. She tries to warn him but before she gets the words out, his head jerks forward violently and a huge sneeze erupts right in her face. There are bits of snot in her hair and on her eyelashes. I can see Jo fighting for composure. She's trying to choose the right words.

'Your mummy wouldn't be very happy with you doing that,' she eventually says, wiping little specks of green from her face.

'My mummy told me to do it!' Boy Two fires back, without missing a beat.

Jo tries to smile. But this time she can't quite manage it.

The class is over. Parents are outside in the corridor, waiting to pick up their children. For a moment, I too look enquiringly up and down the corridor, before I remember I'm supposed to be the one of the parents.

***

As we're driving home, James says he thinks he's had enough of drama. I nod in agreement. Then he asks me if Mummy will be home from work yet. We've had a long day but I can see him slowing down a little, the energy leaking out of him. I tell him that she'll be home soon. When we enter the house, he disappears straight upstairs. Soon he returns carrying a pair of Debs' pyjamas. He is holding them against his face. It seems a bit odd.

'What are you doing, bud?' I inquire softly.

'It's so I can feel Mummy right here beside me until she comes home.'

Children can often infuriate and exasperate the adult mind. But every so often when they get it right, just like great actors, they have that uncanny ability to speak straight to your heart.

Twenty-One

Old Friend

November 2017

The dark-haired waitress raises her eyebrows expectantly at me as she approaches in the cafe.

'I'm waiting for someone – could you just give it a few minutes?' I begin. Then, almost as an apology, I add, 'Well, maybe just bring me a black coffee in the meantime.'

She wanders off without an acknowledgment or a smile. I play with a napkin and study the environment. Small tables pushed close together, presumably to fit in more people. But the cafe is close to empty now and I've picked a remote spot in the corner, my natural instinct being to place myself as far away from other people as I can. I watch pedestrians walking past outside the front window, and wonder if I'll recognise him. It's been many years since we've met and we were never that close anyway.

It's another ten minutes before a tall man enters the room and looks around, as if he hasn't yet decided for certain whether he'll stay. I raise my hand, and he nods and approaches. As we go to greet each other, there's a moment of awkwardness before we settle on a handshake. When I grasp his right hand, he places his left hand on top of mine – a little gesture that takes us slightly past the stilted formality. He sits down opposite me, his features the same as I remember but framed by a heavier face. There's a hint of hardness there, the merest suggestion of tough times. But he's well dressed and assured in his tone, his eyes fixing on mine as he talks evenly, forcing me to look down at the menu.

We order breakfast. A fry for each of us, of course. Then we begin an inane chat about the best places to go for breakfast, why it's an outrage to have beans on an Ulster fry and the fact that nobody from the city knows what you mean when you ask for 'fadge'.

We talk and eat, trying to condense the narratives of more than two decades into a few minutes. We've both got married, raised families and ostensibly been successful in our chosen careers. We show each other photographs of our children on our mobile phones. Then there's a tortured attempt to find some commonality in our youthful memories – shared anecdotes and adventures. But the connection just isn't there, and I'm left feeling that he's reaching for something that never quite existed. A series of hopeful, 'D'ye remember. . ?' questions quickly peter out and hang there between us like stale cigarette smoke in a car. Then there's a silence which is long enough to make us both uncomfortable. Now I think he is beginning to regret coming, as he miserably stirs tea in his cup before going back to the subject of breakfast.

'It's a quare fry.'

'Aye, it is.'

'Quare sausages.'

'Aye.'

'I suppose your wee man is getting big now?'

'Aye, he is. They grow up so fast.'

'Aye, they do.'

'And yours? They're getting big too, I suppose?'

'Aye, they're getting big.'

We nod at each other. I sip my coffee and he sips his

tea. He looks out the window briefly before returning his attention to the mug, and I get the feeling that he's building up to something. Something he hasn't yet decided if he'll share. Then his body seems to tense and his face flushes. For a moment I think he may be in pain, before I conclude the effort is emotional, not physical. Eventually he meets my gaze again.

'Jonny, I asked you to meet me here today because there's something I have to tell you. . .'

This kind of thing has been happening for some months now, ever since I decided to blog, and then talk publicly about my mental health experiences. As I've said, for a while initially I was busy, very busy, dealing with the small rush of correspondence which my story generated. There was a determined swarm of people who wanted to talk to me. I told several that if they had found something familiar in my stories, something of comfort they could grab on to, then that was positive – but, beyond that, I wasn't sure what help I could be. A small number seemed to think that I could cure them. Sadly, I could not and had to tell them so. Jesus, I still had no idea how to cure myself. But I did a lot of listening. It seemed the least I could do if people were prepared to trust me with their darkest fears. I was desperately moved by some of the accounts I heard, and advised several people to seek further help from professionals. But I quickly came to understand that some just wanted to share and found some solace in the fact that someone, who they believed knew what they were going through, was prepared to listen.

But there were also those who wanted to hurt me. Trolling was something I'd quickly had to become used to once I made the decision to speak publicly. One weekend afternoon, when I was enjoying time with my family, I received this message:

I am sick and tired of supposedly grown men like yourself complaining about having tough times. You do not have a mental illness. How dare you lessen such a sickness with your petty complaints about what every adult goes through?

Toughen up, you silly drama queen, Snowflake. The world owes you nothing. Walk in the average man's shoes, you little Snowflake!

This correspondence was not unique – and it was far from the most abusive I'd been sent – but it did make me temporarily doubt the wisdom of speaking out about mental health. I'd known there would be a reaction. What surprised me was the level of the vindictiveness of some of the trolling, the swarm of invective which swelled in my direction. As if admitting that I had a certain weakness was an irresistible invitation for people to pick at that particular scab, to attempt to reopen the wound. The startling realisation that there are a lot of people out there, who will take the time and effort to try and hurt someone they've never met; who will pour so much anger and viciousness into the expression of their opinions.

Naturally, the level of some of the abuse I was subjected to led me to be cautious when dealing with people who reached out to me online. There were those who wanted to meet me, people I'd never set eyes on before, who said they needed to tell me face to face what they were enduring every day in their lives. I struggled for some time, trying to think of an appropriate way to respond to this sort of contact. In the end, and with a feeling of deep uneasiness, I had to decline several offers of meetings. I wasn't qualified to help these people and my own small recovery was still so brittle that I feared a negative experience would shatter it. I also feared someone I didn't know well forming a strong attachment, coming to depend on me and serving me with a burden of responsibility that I could not hope to assume. I simply didn't feel there was enough of me to go around, and that what there was of me wasn't strong enough to be able to take on anyone else's difficulties.

As well as those I'd never met before, several people I'd known earlier in my life got back in touch. I've always been lazy about keeping up personal contacts and have unforgivably allowed more than one friendship to dissolve through lack of care and attention. Now a number of these people seemed to be reappearing.

One day out of the blue I received a message from someone whose name was so dusty in my memory that I almost passed him off as a complete stranger. I had not spoken to or even heard of this person in more than a quarter of a century; moreover, we were never really friends in the first place. There were no shared anecdotes or memories – he was just someone who I had happened to know for a brief spell a very long time ago. And now he was contacting me. I remember his message so well because it was different from all the others. It was short, almost terse, and he gave nothing away about himself: 'Hi, I read what you wrote. Would you be interested in a meeting?'

Chastened by my experiences with trolls, at first, I was unwilling to even reply. After a couple of days however I eventually did respond, committing to nothing and seeing if I could flush out some further information from him. But he continued to tell me nothing more than a few vague details about his career and family. We lived in different parts of the country and worked in different industries. I wasn't sure what the value or point of a meeting would be and told him so. Over the weeks which followed, the correspondence became patchy – but he never quite allowed the thread to break, every now and again sending sporadic, short messages asking after my wellbeing and suggesting a coffee. A couple of times we got as far as arranging a time and place, only for me to back out when more important matters arose. But he kept at it, gently insistent, until it seemed that I had no option left other than to meet the man.

***

And now he sits across from me, building himself up to broach something he clearly needs to talk to me about. I can tell how difficult this is for him so I lean back quietly in my chair, giving him whatever time and room he needs.

'Jonny, I asked you to meet me here today because there's something I have to tell you... I've had my ups and downs in life, just like everybody else. But, Jesus, you're from the same background as me and you know what it's like – if you say anything at all, you're weak. And we're not allowed to be weak. Christ, when I think back on some of the bad days...

'I suppose I found my way of coping – or I thought I had anyway... Then a few months back I came across some of your writing online. It took me a while to even remember who you were. Anyway, I just started reading it. I read it for a long time. Then I went to the bathroom and locked the door and started to cry. I stayed in there for a while, just bawling my eyes out. It went on so long that my wife came to find me. She stood on the other side of that door, begging me to tell her what was wrong. But I just couldn't.

'Eventually I opened the door and she was there. I told her, "I love you and the children more than anything in this world. I would die for all of you but, God help me, I just don't know how to tell you what's going on in my head. I just don't have the words to do it." Then I handed her my laptop and told her, "I want you to read this. Don't ask any questions, just read it. Read it and you'll understand, you'll understand how my mind works and what is going wrong in it. And why I'll never be able to say anything about it."

'She was so scared but she went off and read what was on the screen. I had no idea what she'd do and I was scared too – I suppose I just didn't know what she would think, how she would react. Maybe she'd never be able to look at me as a man again. I sat there on the toilet with my hands shaking until she came back to me. I was terrified but she took my hands and said, "We're going to get you help, and we're going to get it for you tonight. You don't have to be afraid anymore."

'I went to see a doctor that evening and he put me on medication. Now I've got my own psychiatrist and I'm in a support group... It's better than it was. God, there are still plenty of bad days but just . . . just the fact that my wife knows and supports me, and doesn't think any less of me – that's the best part, that's what's really changed things. I never, ever thought I would have that.'

I'm about to mumble some sort of response, but he quickly puts up a hand. He's not quite finished.

'You were probably surprised to hear from me. It certainly wasn't part of my plan to contact you. But my wife said I should do it. Then when you didn't seem that bothered, I wanted to leave it, but she kept at me, telling me that I had to see you. I told her that we weren't even friends but she insisted. When I asked her what was I supposed to say to you, she told me this: "Tell that man that you have a message from me. And the message is this: thank you. Thank you, because if you hadn't shared your story then I'm not sure my husband would be around today."'

Now there's a silence between us. He takes off his glasses for the first time, and I notice the glistening circles of moisture around his eyes. Then I have to look away because I'm afraid he'll set me off. His story raises so many questions, opens so many doors in my mind that I'm desperate to hear more, to squeeze out every drop of information, to learn everything I can from him. But when I look back at him again, I'm sure I see a pleading in his eyes – a pleading for me not to take this conversation any further. I nod my head slowly several times, to let him know that I understand. And to let him know he's done it and it's over. He has said enough.

Then a thought enters my head, a memory from long ago. Now I've remembered – he's a rugby man, a devoted fan. I jump on this like a starving man on a morsel of bread.

'What about Ulster? Do you get to see them much?'

'Ah, not as much as I used to. Sure, they're shocking. Completely gone to the dogs.'

I nod along enthusiastically.

'They haven't been worth a shite since Pienaar left,' I continue.

'That's it. They had it going well, and then they fucked it all up.' He looks deflated now, and he says it again, almost as a whisper. 'They fucked it all up. . .'

Then, suddenly, he checks his watch, and simultaneously we both mumble something about having to be somewhere else. He insists on paying and then follows me back out onto the street, where we have to zip our coats high to protect us from the harsh winter frost. There's no mention of another meeting, or even of staying in touch.

'A bitter one,' I say.

'Aye, it is.'

Then we briefly shake hands before he turns. I watch him as he walks away but the street is thronged with people and it's not long before I can't see him anymore.

Twenty-Two

Being Investigated by Social Services

December 2017

It starts with a letter. Often, I don't open my mail, assuming it to be junk. But this looks like an official correspondence of some kind. The stark white envelope with its serious lettering, addressed to: 'The parents of James McCambridge'. Both of us. I open and read it, but without comprehension at first. Something about a visit to my wife and myself. The letter is from a Health Trust. Social services. I see the letters 'NSPCC'. A lot of things can go through your mind in a short time. My first fleeting thought is that the NSPCC look after animals. I have an absurd moment where I think I am being investigated for cruelty to our goldfish. But then I read it again. Social services have received a referral from the NSPCC. It is about the care of our son, James. They need to talk to his mother and to me. They are coming to our house.

I hold the sheet of paper away from me and study it again. I think I'm looking for an official stamp of some sort. My first belief is that someone must be playing a joke. But the letter has the appearance of authenticity. There is a corporate logo, along with a phone number at the top of the sheet. I call the number and ask for the person who has signed the letter. I'm put on hold and the mellifluous sound of orchestral music fills the receiver. Pachelbel's *Canon*. As I listen to the slow, sweeping strings arrangement I realise,

I think for the first time, that this is actually happening to me.

The music stops and a female voice speaks. Young, I sense, and rather uncertain in her tone. I tell the speaker who I am and she seems to become yet more hesitant, perhaps surprised by the directness of my approach. She confirms that my family is under investigation regarding the care of our son. A complaint has been made to the NSPCC and passed on to social services for consideration. I push her for more detail (such as, what the nature of this complaint is), but she says it is better for these matters to be discussed face-to-face. However, this young social worker does tell me – perhaps in a clumsy attempt at some sort of consolation – that while they need to speak to my wife, she is not under investigation or suspected of any wrongdoing. The allegations (whatever they are) relate solely to myself. She then tells me she will be calling with us the next day and the conversation is ended.

***

There are many ways of thinking about society. Here are a couple:

1. People are inherently good. Yes, there are plenty of bad individuals about, and lots of terrible things happen, but the greater number of us are benign. Society is improving and progressive. We're moving towards a better place than we've come from.

2. Society is just a cover for the brutishness of humanity. More and more terrible things

happen because modern morality is in a state of decay. The growing wickedness of people is taking us into a darker place.

Of course, these are both clumsy generalisations and neither can be exclusively accurate. The truth, as ever, undoubtedly lies somewhere in the middle. Having said that, I know several people whose acquaintance could feed a belief in either theory – individuals who amaze me with their selflessness, or who frighten me with the extent of their cynicism.

I've always aspired towards belonging to the former category. It just seems like a happier way to live. I don't follow any religion, so it's not like I wake up in the morning believing that there has to be a reason for it all. But it just makes it a little easier to rest when I can think that, for my son growing up, the world might be a better place than it was for me. At the same, this makes it all the harder when people let you down.

I'm not well known at all. I do a little bit of blogging but the audience is small. As I've said, I sometimes appear on the radio, where occasionally I'm asked to contribute to a discussion on mental health or parenting. Not as an expert, more as the bumbling mid-life crisis male who can't seem to make sense of anything. That's my niche. It seems that without even trying, I've slipped into the role of a commentator. And when you have any kind of public profile, no matter how insignificant, you inevitably attract some hostility. I've written about the little bit of online trolling I've suffered. The baffling practice of strangers determinedly channelling their energies in an attempt to damage a person they don't even know.

The unleashing of some of this invective, like an angry

dog being let off a chain, has the capacity to scare and disturb. But I've managed to reconcile myself with it. By far the greater number of comments I receive are kind, supportive, loving, even. This takes me back to where I started, and my hope that the majority of people have more good in them than bad.

But it only takes one nasty (or confused, misguided or ill) person to do a bad thing. And what if that person isn't content to limit their actions to merely the anonymous spouting of bile? There have been times when I've wondered what actions such a person might be capable of. And, because of the events I'm about to relate to you, I've now got some idea . . .

***

I'm sitting on the stairs now. Already I can feel legions of negative emotions gnawing at me like moths decimating a piece of long-hidden fabric. There's terror, anger, a huge sadness. . . I sit on my hands to stop them trembling. I have to pick James up from school in less than 20 minutes and I simply can't accommodate a panic attack at this time. I have enough trouble. But then I realise I have to phone Debs and find a way of explaining this. She begins to cry immediately and I find myself in the strange position of trying to console her by explaining that it is my fitness as a parent which is under investigation, not hers. She asks who could have done this to us. It is a question which I will repeat countless times in the hours and days which follow.

I go to the school. I stand there in the playground waiting for my son, surrounded by the other mothers and fathers. Some of them attempt to talk to me but I'm not communicative. I study all the faces, looking for any sign.

James sees me waiting and runs into my arms, burying his face against mine, moistening my cheek with his snot. I hold him, as always, but perhaps for just a little bit longer.

Dinner that evening is a subdued occasion; there seems little to say. When Debs and I do talk about it later, our best conclusion is that a troll must be responsible – someone who has objected to something I have written. The anonymity of this is slightly more comforting than the possibility that it could be somebody we know. A colleague? A fellow parent? A friend?

We go to bed early but sleep is far away. Those who are prone to episodes of depression will know that the terror of exterior forces is dwarfed by the terror of what goes on in your own head. There is no place as genuinely disturbing as your own mind, and tonight the full unvarnished, inglorious, demonic forces are unleashed in mine.

To be clear, I know I have done nothing wrong. I am sure of it. I've given every part of what is good about myself, what is worth anything, in the quest to raise my son in the right way. I pour love and affection in his direction. I always want to make him feel good about himself. I try not to shout at him, and I would cut my own arm off before I raise it in anger against him. He is well fed, properly dressed and groomed, and we try to pack his daily routine with both exercise and stimulation. I throw myself around him as a comfort blanket against all the malign forces in this world.

James is a good-natured, kind and precocious little boy. If I were to admit to any weaknesses as a parent, these would lie in my inability to hold a position of discipline. Sometimes I probably let him get away with too much. That, and my tendency to worry and ruminate excessively.

My insecurities and introspection: the constant feeling that I'm not good enough, along with the awe which fills me at times when I contemplate the size of the task. And my inability to hold something back, and not to give every part of myself to it.

So, as I lie here in bed, thinking about what has occurred, I should have nothing to worry about. But nothing seems certain, in the long dark hours when the thin ray of the streetlight seeps under the bottom of the blinds and casts sinister shapes against the wall. I start to torture myself.

What have I done? Has somebody witnessed something they considered too rough or inappropriate? I play a lot with my son – often in places where there are other kids about. Many times, other children will want to join in and I'm happy to let them. Some of the mothers actually call me 'Fun Daddy'. But has one misinterpreted an action or observed something which made them uncomfortable? Has some mania of parental vigilance in one of them run out of control? Have I clicked on a dubious website in error in an office somewhere? Have I sent my son to school hungry or improperly dressed? I know the answers to all these questions are 'no', but I still search the deepest parts of my mind like some foolish explorer trying to find an elusive Atlantis.

I think about the people I have let into our home. Family and friends who have become close to us and been able to watch us at first hand with our son. Then I think about the facets of myself I have made public, through journalism, social media or broadcasting. I have written and spoken a lot about parenting. Was there something there to make someone think I wasn't up to the job? Now I remember attracting criticism from a small number of parents when I had related an occasion when my son was crying when I left him at crèche. One mother at the time told me she would never be so unfeeling as to leave her child in a state of upset. That had hurt me. I have also written about how James often sleeps in our bed or how I struggle with the processes of discipline. Yet surely none of these are sins grave enough to persuade someone that they should report me? But I have also gone public with my mental health difficulties – the chronic depression, suicidal tendencies and the constant feeling of hopelessness. I did it to try and heal myself. Hopefully, my openness has helped some others as well. But does somebody out there believe that mental health problems and parenting just aren't compatible? That I'm simply not fit to be a father?

I turn over in the bed. There is no comfort to be found. Again and again, I ask myself why this is happening. Is it someone who is misguided, but has a genuine concern about the wellbeing of my son? Or is it something more sinister? A targeted attempt to hurt me? I consider how there is almost a diabolical brilliance in the plan; an intuitive knowledge of where to strike to wound and paralyse me most effectively. Preying on an already fragile mind which is vulnerable to attack. At the heart of my home, with my family. And now there is a question which I cannot get out of my thoughts, which no amount of undeniable logic or rock-hard reason can submerge. . . Is my son going to be taken away from me?

Eventually the longest night gives way to morning. Once I am up and showered and caffeinated, I feel slightly better. In the rush of the day, I know that I can control my fears better than in the still of the night. For the rest of that morning, Debs and I try to keep a routine but we are really just counting down the hours. Eventually, in the early afternoon, I see a small car pulling up outside the house.

The woman is younger than me, perhaps by a dozen or so years, and seems harried. I am unsure of the conventions when meeting someone who is investigating allegations that you're an unfit parent, so I settle for a friendly handshake and the offer of a cup of tea. The handshake is accepted, the tea refused.

My dad has come to the house to look after James while the woman interviews Debs and myself. But the intuition of the very young can be keen, and my boy seems to sense that something different is happening. He clings to my leg, refusing to leave the room.

'Come on, son, go with Granda. Mummy and Daddy just need to talk to the nice woman for a few minutes.'

'No, Daddy! I want to stay here with you!'

Eventually we persuade him from the space and uncomfortably sit staring at each other. The social worker begins by reiterating that the NSPCC have received a complaint. I go through the routine of asking who made it. She tells us she does not know: it has been done anonymously. I am then informed that I am facing 13 allegations. I stare some more. The first, she begins, is that in 1987, in a public place in front of witnesses, I beat up two women. My emotions leap. Partly from the brutality of the accusation, partly because it is so far from the truth. I know it to be absurd. Until this moment I didn't know what this woman would produce from her file. Relief spreads through me like a forest fire. I shouldn't need to be relieved, but somehow, I am.

Then my wife intervenes.

'You do realise that in 1987 my husband would have been 12 years old?'

The woman studies a piece of paper. Then she nods and confirms this fact. She continues reading. . . I have been persistently guilty of domestic violence, beating up my wife and striking my son. I have been known to have trouble controlling my temper and am prone to rage. I suffer from a serious mental illness but I will not seek medical help. I constantly belittle, insult and disparage my son in public. I keep and treat my son like a pet; I am training him like an animal to target my enemies. The list goes on. I listen. Then it is finished. The social worker looks at me. I look back.

'Is there anything you'd like to say, Mr McCambridge, in answer to the allegations? Do you deny them?'

I know what I want to say. . . How have we arrived at a point when this kind of toxicity can be brought into my home? To upset my wife and son in this way?

'Yes,' I respond wearily. 'I deny the allegations; they're entirely false. It's all nonsense.'

I tell her that I have spoken publicly about mental health and parenting. My wife tells her that I am the least likely person to be guilty of the things that I am being accused of. The woman watches us closely. I can't tell if she is being sympathetic or thinking, 'Well, you would say that.' She asks us if she can discuss the case with our GP, as she has some questions for her. Have I been taking my medication? Has my wife ever turned up with any unexplained bruises?

The social worker tells me that if she thinks there is something to be worried about, she also has the option of talking to the police or my child's school. She stresses that all complaints have to be investigated, even if they seem vexatious to us. Debs and I nod along. She tells us she will try to bring the investigation to a swift conclusion – but warns she is drowning in paperwork which could lead to delays. Then she leaves.

And now we try to think what the right thing is to say to each other. My earlier relief is giving way to a deep sense of agitation. My charitable thought – that someone had done this out of a confused sense that it was the right thing – is dead. This has been a long catalogue of mendacity. It is malicious, a deliberate attempt to garrotte me. I have no enemies. Not a single person in the world that I trouble myself to think badly of. But now, this.

My faith in the decency of people has been badly shaken. And I am angry. Angry that I could not do or say any single thing that proves my innocence. Angry that the things I said to the social worker are probably exactly the same as what a guilty man in denial would say. Angry that the stain of accusation, once it is there, can never be entirely removed. Even as I write these words, I think that there'll be someone reading it who is not quite sure of the truth. My upset stays with me for some time. I have another couple of nights of troubled rest with troubled dreams. But every wound heals a little if you give it some time. Soon I start to think less about it.

Some weeks later, I get a phone call from the social worker who had visited our house.

'Mr McCambridge, I just wanted to let you know that we've spoken to your GP and we're closing this investigation. Your doctor backed up everything you said and suggested, quite strongly, that we were barking up the wrong tree.'

And that is it.

But emotions, questions and fears cannot be shut down as simply as an investigation. The hurt cannot be undone. And I'm left with the queasy realisation that someone out there dislikes me enough to do this. And if they'll do this, then what else will they do? Even worse, I've no idea who did it. I never will. I have to stop myself from looking suspiciously at every acquaintance. Only madness lies down that road. The process of the investigation – the coldness of the letter, the necessity to tell my family, the waiting, the uncertainty and fear about the outcome, the humiliation of the accusation – all of these things combined have made for one of the worst experiences of my life. One which has pushed me back towards the darkness, closer than it's safe for me to go. But then, maybe that was the point?

Sometimes in life you get what you deserve. But sometimes you don't. Yet I'm through it now, and I'm not angry anymore. I'm moving on as before. Bad things happen, but the power of humanity for me is in trying not to allow the wickedness, when I see it, to possess or alter me. And not allowing it to diminish my capacity for hope.

Jonny McCambridge

Part Three

Jonny McCambridge

Twenty-Three

Return to Work

February 2018

It's a charcoal winter morning. A hard frost has layered itself onto the pavements, a ubiquitous shining spider's web. My car engine rumbles impatiently, like breathing which is not quite even. I pull quietly onto the motorway. I raise a hand to acknowledge the driver who let me in, but I'm not sure if he sees me. This bothers me for a moment and I wonder if I should wave again. It's early, traffic is not a problem yet, but it's dark and the roads are slippery. It's the first time I've driven in the dark this winter and I worry about whether the headlights are working properly.

The traffic moves easily and I'm driving automatically without noticing anything. I try to force myself to concentrate on the road, mentally marking every bright sign and dark tree that I pass. But I can't keep it up and soon my attention drifts away like a line of smoke from a chimney pot. I don't feel great; my stomach is cramping and ripples of anxiety wash through my body. Today will be the first time I'll be working in an office since I quit my job as a journalist 18 months ago.

Actually, it's not as permanent or impressive as I just made it sound. The editor of a small trade magazine has asked me to help out in her office with a bit of writing. A few days of work to begin with. We'll see how it goes, she said. And it's not even full days – I'm only working until lunchtime. I told her I have to be finished in time each day to pick my son up from school. I know what the work will be – rewriting press releases, maybe making a few phone calls for quotes; filling little spaces in the magazine as they arise. It's the sort of journalism I started out doing a quarter of a century ago, and the other side of the world from working at the top of a daily newspaper, being the one making the decisions.

But recently I've been aware of the need for me to get some money coming into the house. Months of staying at home has helped my damaged mind to begin to repair, but it's shredded the delicate health of my bank balance. Although I've been trying not to dwell on it, I can't get away from the glaring and obvious truth that the sums just don't add up anymore. I've never been much good with money, always allowing it to slip through my fingers and then puzzling over why I have nothing to show afterwards. But while I was in a well-paid job, I was able to keep an approximate balance between what was coming in and going out. Even if I overstretched myself, I knew there was always another pay slip on the way. But not now. Debs is still earning but it's not enough and I know that I need to contribute too. Lately another chilling question has invaded my brain and gnaws away relentlessly at my thoughts when I can't sleep or when I have a quiet moment – what happens when the money runs out? The potential humiliation of not being able to pay the bills, of not living up to the very basic expectation that a father should support his children, now drives most of my thoughts.

In recent months, I've been doing bits and pieces of work – a few freelance jobs and writing or training assignments – but it's been nowhere near enough to plug the leaks in this ship. And the brutal truth is that the phone hasn't been ringing. The trade magazine is the first thing anyone's offered me in a while and I'm in no position to refuse. I'd always said that I would begin to look for a job again when James started school, but the time has gone so quickly and I honestly just don't feel ready to step back into work in an office. But yet, here I am.

I'm getting dangerously close to Belfast so I slow the car down, as if this will somehow delay the day's work. All the old hateful feelings are back. The fear that nobody will like me; that I won't be able to do the work; that they'll laugh at me; that I won't fit in. That I'll never fit in. I shift in the car seat; I know it shouldn't be this way. After all, this is the closest thing yet to what I've been looking for: flexible hours that I can fit around childcare, no real pressure, no responsibility. The work should be easy. Yet there's a burning deep in my throat and I can taste the juices of my own vomit which I have to keep forcing back down. I think I know what's wrong. It's the feeling of reality crashing around me like waves at the wall of a pier. The reality of the incivility of civilisation.

The truth is that I've enjoyed my time away from the grind of work and being outside the system. Spending time with my wife and James, devoting my life to making sure my son's is all that it can be. But I always knew it couldn't last, because the money headache never goes away. It's the Monday morning bleakness, the despair and suffocation of the forced routine. My life being ordered into a relentless series of fives and twos, fives and twos. Knowing that if I leave a problem, it will still be there the next morning when I get to my desk. It's just the sheer grimness of the whole shabby process.

I steer my car off Tates Avenue onto the Lisburn Road and pull up outside the little office. I was so worried about being late that I've ended up getting here more than an hour before it opens. This sounds extreme but it's quite usual for me. The office is in darkness, the door locked.

I might as well go for a walk. I decide to find a coffee shop. It's not so much that I'm desperate for caffeine but rather that my insides are in turmoil and I'd feel better just knowing I'm somewhere close to a toilet. Turning up on the first morning having shat myself is not the best way to make a good impression. It's still dark but the streetlamps and headlights of the cars make the rain shine on the road and footpaths.

I used to live in this part of the city, more than 20 years ago when I was at university. I'm trying to find any shop that I remember but they're nearly all gone or closed. Streets change faster than people do. I'm looking for a cafe and there are many here but it's so early that they're not open yet. I walk past a line of people, heads down, waiting at a bus stop. I think about how this is the first morning that I have not been there to take James to school, to watch him stumble uncertainly into the playground, turning briefly to give me that little wave and nod of the head before he scurries off around the corner. For a moment I feel a desperate weakening and fear that I might cry.

I'm about to give up when I spot a coffee shop with the lights on. It's part of a chain, a brand name that I see all over Belfast these days. I'd sooner have an independent shop, although I'm not sure why. I enter the shop. It's brightly lit, full of soft black and brown sofas and tall chairs. The gentle sound of Enrico Einaudi's piano music fills the space, and I'm encouraged. I take a bottle of sparkling water from a cold cabinet to the counter. There a young woman with short brown hair greets me with a genuine and warm smile, displaying a row of white teeth and dark eyes. I'm a little disconcerted. Maybe it's because

I'm not in a very good mood, maybe it's because I'm not used to being addressed in such a pleasant way by a staff member in a coffee shop. She's Eastern European.

I order a coffee and we make a faltering attempt at conversation but I think she's struggling to understand my Ulster-Scots drawl so I abandon it. I take my coffee and find a comfortable chair. I've bought a newspaper but I don't feel like reading it now. Instead, I watch the woman behind the counter. I'm slightly embarrassed that I can't be any more specific than to say she sounds Eastern European. I wonder where she's from, what her story is. She meets every customer with that same smile and attempts to chat with them all. Some of the customers are clearly regulars and she holds a conversation with each one, as she carefully pours steaming coffee into delicate white cups, before balancing these on saucers.

I'm enjoying the sound of Einaudi as I sip at my coffee and nibble on my nails, making the ends of my fingers ache. I haven't been aware of the change occurring but I notice now that I'm feeling a bit better. I watch a couple at the table next to me – at least I'm assuming they're a couple because they don't speak to each other. She's trying to eat a croissant in a dignified way, brushing flakes of pastry off her skirt as delicately as if she was stroking a baby's face. His eyes never leave the broadsheet paper he holds in one hand, even when he reaches for his coffee with the other. His fingers search for the handle of the cup.

A small car pulls up outside the shop, but it's still too dark to identify which make or colour. Two girls in a dark school uniform step out of the front seats and enter. They order drinks and then have a brief discussion about whether to sit in or have them to go. They pay by card and present their loyalty cards to be stamped before they leave the shop. Sitting near me there's a middle-aged woman wearing a long dark skirt and a pair of glasses on a chain, reading a book, a large hardback which looks like it might have been borrowed from a library. I strain my eyes to make out the title but she's not holding it upright enough. I keep trying and soon she looks up, catching my eye with a disapproving scowl, and I quickly glance out of the window, into the rain.

All at once there's a commotion on the other side of the shop and I turn my head. Two men, both short in stature, are shouting. Both are wearing similar blue overalls and I assume they are work colleagues. One is sitting at a table waving a newspaper while the other stands over him, yelling aggressively. I notice his hands are tightly gripped into fists and his torso is thrust forward. I think he's about to hit the seated man. Everyone in the shop is watching them now. But then the standing man grabs a large plastic cup of coffee from the edge of the table and storms away, mumbling angrily. I keep watching him as he walks past and soon his eyes meet mine.

'What are you staring at, wanker?' he barks bitterly.

I don't answer and return my gaze to the coffee, which is now cold in the white cup. The man hurriedly leaves the shop. I wait for a few minutes and then go to the toilet where I have a painful bout of diarrhoea. I wash my hands, taking time to scrub each finger, working carefully to clean what is left of my fingernails before I throw water onto my face. I examine myself in the mirror. I look old, too old to be starting over. I check my phone, there's a message from Debs: *Good luck. You know you can do this. Love you xxx.*

I go back outside and leave the shop. It's that time between darkness and light, and a half-light is starting to break through. It's time for me to go to work.

Twenty-Four

The School Run

March 2018

I haul myself out of bed. I can't say I've just woken up, as that would suggest that I'd actually been asleep in the first place. Rather, I've just summoned the energy to pull myself upright. Or close to upright. It's a day when I'm not working in the office in the job I started recently. It is going ok – at least I haven't made any obvious errors. The boss seems happy enough, although when I asked her about the possibility of getting more days, she said she'd have to see how things go. So, for today, it's back to the school run.

It's 7.45 a.m. – and we have to be out of the house by 8.15 a.m. If I wasn't so tired, I'd be starting to panic now. Yes, if I was clear-headed enough to think about all of the things which need to be done in the next 30 minutes, I'd be really panicking. It's like writing a news story right up against deadline. If you stop to think about it, then you simply wouldn't be able to do it. I look at my son, still sleeping. Mouth open, eyes closed. He ended up clambering into our bed at some point in the night. Again. He woke us up a couple of times in the early hours looking for a drink, then needing the toilet. At one point he was lying on top of me, his feet resting on my face. At another point he moaned, 'Daddy, you're squashing me', as he sprawled out on the bed and I was banished to the Siberian cold outer edges of the mattress.

Now, of course, he's sleeping sweetly. Now that I need him to be washed, breakfasted and dressed. I decide to shower before he's awake. The water is tepid, naturally. You could argue that if we were a normal family, the night before we'd have set the alarm, set the timer to warm the water, had the schoolbag packed, the clothes ready. If we were a normal family. I come back into the bedroom. Debs is sorting through piles of clothes. I presume there's a point to this. James is climbing out of bed, hair like leftover spaghetti.

He smiles. 'Is it morning already?'

It's cute. But a little sinister too – like he knows too much. Is it a smile, or a smirk? I give him a hard stare. I try to rush him downstairs for breakfast. But in my haste, I've forgotten his toy light sabre. I lose another minute running back to get it. Everybody knows you can't have breakfast without your light sabre. I go through the routine of trying to get him to eat something healthy.

'Do you want some fruit?'

'Honey Monsters.'

'Maybe an apple?'

'Honey Monsters.'

'I could peel it and slice it up?'

'Honey Monsters.'

'Or I could make a smoothie? I've got some lovely fresh strawberries.'

'Honey Monsters.'

I think for a second.

'Ok, you can have Honey Monsters today because we're late, but tomorrow you're going to have something healthy. You can't have Honey Monsters every day.'

I ponder my own breakfast. The array of cereals in the cupboard. Fresh fruits in the fridge. Nuts and seeds. I decide I'll have Honey Monsters too. But James won't start eating until the TV is on. I fumble with the remote control, my thick fingers bouncing off the buttons like King Kong trying to play a harpsichord. There used to be a time when you pushed a switch and the TV started to work. A simpler time. Now you have to endure a seemingly endless process where the telly seems to be somehow warming up. A taunting message keeps flashing on the screen: 'Nearly there. . . nearly there. . . nearly there . . .' And then the screen goes blank again. When I was a kid, you had five minutes of children's TV a day, and you felt grateful. My son insists on his favourite programme. His favourite episode of his favourite programme. His favourite scene from his favourite episode of his favourite programme. And then, finally, we can eat.

I run upstairs with a cup of tea for Debs. She's still doing something with clothes.

'Where's the wee man's uniform?' she challenges me.

'How would I know?'

'Well, you took it off him last night.'

'No I didn't.'

I know I did but sometimes you just have to hold the line. I glance at the top of the laundry basket, where I always throw clothes in a crumpled pile. The uniform isn't there. We go into the spare bedroom. His uniform is laid out neatly on the bed, with clean underwear and socks. The advantage has moved to me – Debs clearly did this before bedtime but has forgotten. But for her to admit it now would be to concede she was the last one to touch the uniform.

'There you go,' I declare insufferably, 'just where I left everything.'

She lets me have the moment. Then she thrusts the uniform at me.

'Well, you can get him dressed then.'

I trudge back down the stairs. It's part dressing, part all-in wrestling. With Honey Monsters thrown in. I'm gently encouraging him. 'Come on, son, you should be putting on your own socks by now.'

He's bashing me over the head with his light sabre, and not gently. But somehow, he ends up dressed.

'We're all ready! How're you getting on?' I shout up the stairs to Debs. A hint of triumphalism and challenge in my voice.

'Is he washed? Has he brushed his teeth? Are his shoes and coat on? Have you packed his snack?'

I don't respond. I wash his face roughly with a flannel like I'm cleaning graffiti off a wall.

'Too rough, Daddy!' he tries to protest, but his mouth is full of facecloth.

I turn my attention to his lunchbox. I have to come up with a healthy snack for James every day. This is a boy who regards chocolate raisins as a health food. There's a note from the school at the bottom of the schoolbag. It says some of the children have allergies, so we should avoid sending in anything which contains nuts or egg. I stare at it. My plans for a cashew and pecan frittata have just crashed down around me. I put some breadsticks and a little box of raisins in his schoolbag.

Then it's shoes. I've been able to put my own shoes on now for . . . I don't know . . . 40 odd years, but putting someone else's shoes on seems to throw me. James gives me the usual warning.

'Put them on the right feet, Daddy. Check they're on the right feet, Daddy. Are they on the right feet, Daddy?'

'Look, I've only sent you out with your shoes on the wrong feet once!' I growl back.

'You did it twice, Daddy.'

'Ok, well, I've put them on the right feet more often than the wrong ones.'

Debs comes down the stairs as I finish tying his laces. I think we're ready to go now but instead she's looking for envelopes in the kitchen.

'What are you doing?'

'We have to send in these reply slips for the teacher.'

'Why didn't you do this last night?' I say, without a hint of irony in my voice.

'Why didn't you?'

I think about this. To say that I didn't because I was watching the snooker seems to lack authority, so I shut up. Then I notice her slipping money into one of the envelopes.

'What's that for?' I protest.

'To buy some stuff for his art projects.'

'What do I pay my taxes for?'

The pedant could point out that as I've been out of work for the last 18 months, I haven't actually been paying any taxes, but we're against the clock here. Finally, we're ready for the car. I lock the front door. At this exact moment, just as I do every day, I realise I've forgotten to take my pills. I rush back inside and hurriedly down the little white tablets with a glass of water. Then I run back outside and start the car.

At this point James says, 'I need the toilet!'

For a moment nobody says anything. Then my wife speaks.

'Did Daddy not check if you needed the toilet before you left the house, son?'

'No, Mummy.'

As she takes him back towards the house, I shout out the window, 'We're already late, so blaming people now isn't going to help us or get us to school any faster.'

I sit back, thinking that I've slightly softened the edges of my defeat. Soon they're back in the car and I'm driving faster than I should, flashing my lights and beeping my horn in the school carpark to get children and mummies with prams to move out of my way. As we take our son through the gates, I notice I've put his coat on inside out. I decide to let it go. He'll be taking it off in a few seconds anyway. We take him to the door. We're not even the last ones there. We kiss him goodbye and walk away, leaving him in the care of his teacher. Just like any other family.

Twenty-Five

The Academic

August 2018

It's early and I'm awake. I'm never much of a sleeper but the pitiless heat of this summer has led to endless nights of constantly turning and shifting in search of elusive comfort of some kind. I'm lying on my back on top of the covers, watching my stomach slowly rise and fall, dissatisfied at the sight of my own shape. Debs and James are stretched out beside me, like figures in a painting of a shipwreck. They're both asleep and breathing placidly. I reach for my watch and strain to focus my eyes on the thin, black screen. It's between five and six in the morning, and the sun is already filling the room.

I'm exhausted but I pull myself upright, every muscle screaming out for more rest. I walk into the next room. The spare bedroom. It's stuffy in here and the air is like lead in my lungs. There is mess everywhere – discarded clothes, papers and toys – which makes it difficult for my feet to find the ground. The sight fills me with despair. I move to the little desk I have placed beside the window. There's sun here as well and the seat of the chair is warm, like bread just out of the oven. It's a makeshift operation and in order for my legs to fit under the desk, I have to roll the chair back, using my weight to push it against the bed to clear space.

I turn on the computer and it scratches and purrs reluctantly to life. While I wait for all the applications to open, I look out the window and notice the garden shed. From this height I can see the area where the roof has collapsed, with a tangle of vines stretching down into the ugly dark hole. Replacing the shed: it's a job I've been meaning to do for several months, but my inability to focus on the logistics of the work, as well as the financial commitment, have meant it has not been achieved. Looking at that hole, it occurs to me now, is like staring at a representation of my own failures. This thought, and the disorder of the room around me, leads to a familiar darkness beginning to flood my mind, relentlessly moving forward and twisting around me, just like the vines. All at once I feel overwhelmed by it – unable to cope, muscles flooded with anxiety.

I force myself to focus once more on the computer screen, opening emails and rolling the mouse under my trembling fingers. I know what I need to do – I've been here enough times before. Divert myself, pull myself roughly in a different direction so the dust of a bad day cannot begin to settle around me. I begin to make a list of the things I have to do and look at my watch again. I've probably got less than two hours before James and Debs are awake, before the meandering path of the day takes me away from here. I have to get on.

This is my life now. In my previous working life, I fitted my family around my job. Now any efforts at paid work fill out the cracks of my domestic existence. My thoughts turn once more to the need to make money, to try to balance out how much I'm spending. But I force myself not to think too far ahead, aware of the potentially destabilising effect of the big picture. Finding new employment opportunities has been tough. I usually insist on working from home so I can maximise my time with

James, but this limits how much I can reasonably undertake. The truth is that I'm hardly in demand. Aside from my part-time work on the trade magazine, I'll get the occasional request to write a feature or newspaper article, or to make a rare broadcast appearance when they can find nobody else to go on, as well as little bits of editing and proofing work for publications every now and again. Some months I make a little money, but it's never really enough.

I click the mouse arrow onto a miniature yellow folder and a white spreadsheet fills the computer screen. I've modified it so it works as a basic page plan, representing the draft layout of a magazine. This is some work I've brought home with me that I need to get finished before I'm next in the office of the magazine. I'm keen to do a good job, hoping that if I impress them, they might give me some more hours.

People often tell me these days how well I'm doing; how good I'm looking. How I'm a different guy than I was before. But I know that any veneer of recovery is as thin as tracing paper and liable to tear at the first sign of friction. And there's a new hidden difficulty which this job on the magazine has revealed. It's the kind of work where I'm required to deal with other people – carrying out interviews, commissioning writers, communicating with advertisers. After almost two years of being at home I'm now able to see how much I've withdrawn into myself and how far away I have travelled from the accepted forms of socialisation. Now, the act of making a simple professional phone call fills me with a crippling terror; the routine sending of an introductory email reduces me to a state of panicked incoherence. Simple tasks, which I should be able to complete quickly, are routinely put off for days and

I'm only too aware that this is the enemy of organised editing.

But I have to force myself through it, to find a way to manage. I flick through a couple more emails. I haven't smoked in a long time but the very act of sitting in front of a computer always triggers something latent within me which makes me long for a cigarette. I write a couple of articles quickly, just rehashing press releases to create filler material. But eventually I have to look at the page plan again, to confront the problem I've been desperate to avoid. The magazine is close to complete, but there's a large gap in the middle, a space set aside for a long feature. I've commissioned an academic to contribute an article on his area of research. But he's late, more than a week late.

It's not feasible to pull or replace the feature now because a large amount of advertising revenue has been sold on the back of it appearing, and it's too close to deadline to think of finding someone else to write it. All of my phone calls and most of my emails to the academic have been unanswered. He has only responded with a couple of terse notes, the first claiming that he had a 'family emergency' and then later, 'an upset tummy'. I don't believe him and know that I'm being given the run-around. I'm half-angry at being let down and half-afraid at the prospect of a confrontation. I allow a wave of defeatism to roll over me. *It's always the same when you rely on other people, they always fucking let you down.*

I begin to compose an email. I think about tone of voice, wanting to sound friendly but professional, supportive while highlighting the urgency of the situation. In the end I type it quickly.

I hope you are feeling better – you've had a rough time by the sounds of it. I just wanted to enquire about how the feature is coming on. I know you've had things going on but we're now well past the agreed date. If I don't see the article soon then we're going to miss deadline and this could hold up the production of the magazine. Let me know how you are progressing. Best regards . . .

I send the message and sit back, blowing out my cheeks as if I've achieved something substantial. I can hear Debs in the bathroom now, preparing for her day at work. Work at a proper job. I send off a few more emails before I hear the familiar small footsteps behind me. I turn to see James, all blond hair and crumpled pyjamas, a fleck of fear in his eyes.

'Daddy, I woke up, and you and Mummy weren't there.'

'Hi buddy, it's ok, I was just doing a bit of work and Mummy's getting ready for the office.'

'Is it school today, Daddy?'

'No buddy, you're on school holidays now, did you forget?'

His pale little face brightens, the beginning of a smile.

'Are you looking after me today?'

'Of course I am.'

'Are we going to have adventures?'

'Yes, we are.'

He steps closer to me. Now I notice he's holding a teddy under one arm.

'Can I write something on your computer, Daddy?'

'Yes you can, son.'

***

It's late now. It's one of those fine summer evenings when the clouds roll in at leisure, reddened by the heavy sun, until a warm and still dusk has descended. I'm upstairs, back at the computer. I've had another full day with James, struggling as ever to come up with ideas on how to keep him entertained, giving all of my energy to him and wondering what will be left for myself. Then, after he goes to bed, I spend a couple of hours watching TV and chatting with Debs, keeping to our routine of making some time for each other, hearing her stories from the newsroom. Then, once she goes to sleep, I go back to work.

The first thing I do is check the emails, scanning them quickly until I see the name which has been on my mind for most of the day. The academic who has kept me waiting. An email is there but I quickly notice there is no attachment and I'm instantly deflated, knowing that the work has still not been sent and another excuse is coming. The frustration is almost seeping out of my fingers as I open the message, thoughts and accusations crowding my mind more quickly than I can process them. I read the email.

Dear Jonny – thank you so much for your message and for your understanding. I am so sorry to have kept you waiting. The truth is – and this is something that I have told very few people – that I have suffered a major depressive episode. When this happens, it is very difficult for me to work and I have not been able to get out of bed for several days. My doctor has advised me against working at the moment, but I am hopeful that I will be feeling better soon and will be

able to complete the work you have commissioned.
Once again, please accept my apologies, even the
mere task of writing this message has exhausted me.
Best regards. . .

I read the email a few times, taking my time over each line.
I close it and try to start another task, but soon I find
myself opening the message once more. I'm agitated and I
have to get up, walking out of the room, down the stairs
and into the back yard. I go to the small, paved area at the
bottom of the garden where I like to sit in my old chair.

I rest and watch the dark outlines of the tall trees, the
slightest whisper of the wind making the tips of the
branches move gently. You can only see this if you stop and
take the time to look. I don't know what I'm feeling or quite
how to express it. Emotions don't always present
themselves in a clear and easily defined form as a writer
might like them to, but instead can be smudged and
muddled, like colours that have run into each other.
Perhaps I'm a little ashamed, a little angry, a little worried,
a little lost. I'm also desperate for a cigarette.

I sit there until my backside is numb and the area at
the back of my knees begins to ache. I think of many nights
I have sat here before, on my own. Then I rise and go back
into the house, up the stairs and into my makeshift office.
I've no stomach for work now but I have one thing I need
to do before I finish. I compose an email to a man I have
never met:

Thank you so much for responding to me and I am so
sorry if I have done anything to make you feel worse.
Do not worry at all about the feature – I will find
another way. Please do what your doctor says and

take all the rest and time you need. If you ever need someone to talk to, then please contact me at any time. Please take care.'

I read the email over. I'm about to send it, but I stop and decide to add another line:

There is always help out there and better times ahead. Please never feel that you are alone.

I send the message and quickly turn off the computer, not wanting to think about doing any other work tonight. I brush my teeth and go into the bedroom. Because of the heat, Debs has left the small window open, and I can hear the low roar of cars from the nearby motorway. There's a little bedside lamp that we leave on because James is afraid of the dark. I kiss my sleeping wife and son and climb on top of the bed. I hope to Christ that I too will be able to get some sleep tonight.

Twenty-Six

Post-Christmas Blues and the Wobbly Tooth Redemption

January 2019

The vapidity of these days is, I suppose, to be expected. Christmas is over. Done. We're in that strange in-between time. School and work have yet to recommence and the days pass now with none of the intoxication of before. I feel trapped in their dreary emptiness while simultaneously dreading the crushing, imminent return to grey normality.

For me, it's always like this in the early part of January. After the interminable build-up, Christmas passes as fast and slippery as a young fish and all that is left is some familiar sense of regret over the inexorable, grinding progression of the clock.

Those who live with the vulnerability of susceptibility to depression will know of the danger of the dark January days. In December, the bleakness of a cold, red morning horizon is filled with enchantment. In January it can reek of hopelessness. Perhaps this is because during Christmas, the defences have been temporarily lowered, the mind and body surrendered to a state of abandon. Perhaps it is simply because endings are easier than beginnings. Whatever is the case, the worries and the weight of my responsibilities leak back into my thoughts, spreading like mould.

The new toys are still scattered on the carpet of the 'good' room. The Christmas tree is there in the corner. I haven't found the will to take it down but have no desire to see the lights. That's where I am, stranded, unable to summon the energy to do anything new even though I am tired of what has gone before.

As I said, it's a dangerous time and I know the trick is to bring focus and order to the mind. To give myself a task. To bring some kind of mystical importance to what would otherwise be inane. Don't let the sense of rot set in.

Today it is the bins. The gloriously comforting, dependable routine of the bins. Sorting the surplus of rubbish into piles for the green, brown and blue receptacles. I'm tearing cardboard boxes to pieces and crushing cans and plastic bottles as I challenge myself to fit more and more in. I find myself slipping into a familiar obsessive state as I go through every individual piece of waste, making sure it is in the right bin. Soon I'm removing labels from plastic containers and washing them, taking time to ensure that every small particle of food is removed from the most elusive corners. I think I may even be smiling as I consider that basically what I'm doing is washing my rubbish.

It's just James with me in the house today – Debs has already returned to work. We play superhero games which consist of me chasing him around the house, only to be bashed on the head with a pillow when I catch him. It seems to go on for a long time. In truth the game feels a little bit flat, and I wonder is it possible that even children can grow tired of having too much empty time. Then he wants to watch a film so I leave him in the front room while I go upstairs. I try to read but find I cannot concentrate on the words. I'd love to write something but I know that it's when I try too hard to reach a creative state that I'm least likely to find it.

So instead, I just lie on the bed, wandering somewhere deep inside my own mind. I know I'm not depressed or anxious right now, but I'm concerned that I'm heading in that direction. So I just concentrate on being self-aware. Trying, as ever, to understand all of the layers and processes within my own head. I can't stop thinking about how fine the lines are between a healthy mental state and something much darker.

Then I hear James coming up the stairs. My first emotion, I'm ashamed to say, is one of weariness. I'm anticipating another long bout of superhero role-playing. *Aw, buddy, just let Daddy have five more minutes*, I rehearse internally as I hear him approaching the bedroom. But when he comes through the door, his face is flushed and serious – a child trying to replicate what he imagines is an adult expression. I sit up immediately as he begins to speak.

'Daddy, there's something I have to tell you. Something I need you to check.'

'What is it, buddy? Are you alright?'

His face is creased with the effort of processing new thoughts and experiences.

'Daddy, I think I might have a wobbly tooth.'

He wants me to look in his mouth. Eventually I manage to persuade him that he needs to remove his finger and move his tongue – and then I see it. A tiny pearl-like tooth in the bottom row which is dangling by a thread. It must have been loose for some time but he has only just realised what is happening.

'Yes, buddy, you definitely have a wobbly tooth. That's going to fall out soon.'

And then it begins. The pleasure overtakes his tiny body and he begins to bounce, as he always does when excited. 'I can't believe it, Daddy. I can't believe I have my first wobbly tooth.'

He talks like this with animation for some time. He begins to tell me about every person in his class at school, naming them individually as he recites how many wobbly or missing teeth they have had – a complete juvenile dental record of all of his friends. He has never spoken to me on this subject before but now I'm aware of how it must have dominated his thoughts and the discussions in the playground. How often must he have wondered when it was going to be his turn? Children's minds, just like those of adults, are full of unspoken mysteries and surprises.

We talk of the Tooth Fairy, and I find his joy and wonder spreading into me like a contagion. It's only a tooth but it means so much more to him. He seems to be more excited in this moment than he was at any time over Christmas. Perhaps more excited than I've ever seen him before. He keeps repeating a couple of lines over and over.

'I can't believe I've got a wobbly tooth. I'm a big boy now!'

Perhaps there should be some pathos in this process, as my boy takes another step towards growing up, another step away from me, but I can't help but be carried along with his excitement and pure, undiluted happiness. He is desperate to tell his mummy. In his world, no experience is complete unless it is shared entirely with her. I tell him I'll get her on the phone but he wants to wait – to tell her in person, to do it properly and with due ceremony. So, we wait, and play more games, but now the previously elusive sense of animation and adventure has returned.

Occasionally James stops just to give me one of his smiles and I'm aware of how the romantic notions of my child have swept away my usual mundane worries – and how much better I am for it.

Eventually Debs comes home. I have to bring her into the front room and ask her to sit down, so that our son can make his announcement. There are tears and hugs. A little later, Debs puts him to bed but it is some time before he is calm enough to sleep. Afterwards she tells me that as he lay there, he kept repeating the same two lines, over and over, in a whisper: 'I can't believe I've got a wobbly tooth – I'm a big boy now. I can't believe I've got a wobbly tooth – I'm a big boy now. . .'

***

The next morning, there is momentary panic. The tooth is gone, leaving only a dark gap at the bottom of his mouth. Soon Debs finds it on the mattress. She holds it in the palm of her hand and we both stare, astonished by how small and white it is – like a delicate jewel or even a tiny, distant star. Tiny and pearly white, but able to brighten the darkest of January days.

Twenty-Seven

Sports Day

June 2019

The early spring sun is strengthening and burning off the hazy morning dew as we arrive at the school field. The smell of freshly cut grass intoxicates the senses, bringing back memories of my own childhood. The painted white lines on the bumpy grass track are more or less straight. Several things surprise me. The trailer in the corner, with a barista making and selling proper coffee; the huge number of plastic folding chairs set out in rows for parents; the sound system blaring out the music from the *Rocky* film, and the poster explaining that the event is sponsored by a local retail company. School sports day has changed a lot since I was a kid.

But there's a troubling familiarity here also. The anticipation of competition floats in the air this morning, descending on us like pollen, and I feel the same twist of anxiety that used to be there in my youth. Now I'm just a spectator, but no less nervous. James has not yet shown any aptitude for or interest in sports. I know he's not the fastest or the strongest; he's definitely not the most confident. And as starting time comes closer, scenarios of disaster begin to gather in my mind.

What if all the noise and commotion overwhelm him? What if he gets upset because he's not one of the best? What if the trauma makes him hate taking part in competitive games? What if . . . what if? But while I'm wasting time worrying if he's going to be ok, he's too busy being ok to notice. Earlier this morning, when I tentatively asked him about the races, he recited a practised line, something they must have been taught in class: 'It doesn't matter where you finish, Daddy, as long as you have fun.'

Soon it's time to begin. The children are led out by their teacher and I quickly spot James, looking smaller in the line than he seemed when we had dropped him at the gates an hour earlier. His P2 class all sit on a small wooden bench as they wait to be summoned for the first race. Debs and I are frantically waving until he sees us and jumps to his feet, giving us an enthusiastic little shake of his fist. I keep asking Debs, 'Do you think he'll be ok?', over and over until she's forced to pretend she can't hear me anymore.

The egg-and-spoon race is first. The children line up nervously like suspects in a police identity line-up. Then a man in a brown tracksuit blows a whistle and they begin to move. It's only an egg-and-spoon race, but in my mind it becomes a parable for life, a metaphor which reveals the personality of all the children. Some are clearly competitive and move at speed, risking dropping the little ball off their spoons and occasionally kicking it along the grass with their toes when it does fall. James is different. He is at going at walking pace. A slow walking pace. His little face is creased with concentration and effort, determined that he is going to keep the ball on the spoon. He won't take any risks or do anything reckless. He makes it about three quarters of the way down the track before the ball drops. It's between his feet and he struggles to pick it up, perhaps unnerved by all the cheering and clapping coming from the parents.

My mind goes back to 1992 and the Barcelona Olympics. British athlete Derek Redmond was competing in the semi-finals of the 400 metres track race. Once considered a brilliant prospect, Redmond's career had been blighted by injury and the Barcelona games were considered his last chance for athletic glory. He was halfway down the back straight and running beautifully when it happened. Suddenly he collapsed onto the track in agonising pain as his hamstring tore. The race carried on as he lay there, sobbing in agony. As a teenager, I watched the race live and I remember clearly what happened next. Redmond climbed back to his feet and began to try to run again, despite having only one working leg. Race officials attempted to remove him from the track but he was insistent: he was going to finish his Olympic adventure. Then, just as it was becoming apparent that his mission was hopeless, a remarkable thing happened. A slightly overweight man wearing a Nike T-shirt and shorts burst out of the crowd and onto the track. It was Derek Redmond's father. He gathered his inconsolable son in his arms and supported him all the way to the finish line while the crowd stood, wept and cheered.

This all happened a quarter of a century ago, but the anguished, haunted look on the Olympic runner's face comes to me now as I watch my son fumbling on the grass, desperately trying to recover the ball. Perhaps I make an involuntary motion because my wife puts her hand on my arm to calm me. James eventually puts the ball back on the spoon and completes the race. He has finished last. As he is being led back to his bench, he looks at Debs and me. He is smiling.

The programme of races continues and our boy is not anywhere near the front of any of them. But he keeps smiling and I keep shouting and telling him how wonderful he is, and trying to stop myself from invading the track like Derek Redmond's father. I'm expending loads of nervous energy, yelling encouragement, and every couple of minutes he looks over to give Debs or myself a shy wave or a thumbs-up. At one point while the sound system is playing Europe's 'The Final Countdown', I could swear he's dancing. And he just keeps on smiling while the sun gets higher.

At a certain point, the headmaster reads out the names of all the little boys and girls who have won the races so far. Our son is not among them. The next, blue riband event is the sprint race. But it's only for selected children who have been deemed fastest in trials held on a previous day. James is not one of the chosen competitors and I'm a little wounded – stung that he's been made to go through a process and judged not good enough to compete. While the sprint goes on, I watch him on the bench, picking blades of grass and little daisies out of the ground.

The final event is a relay of sorts. A team race with obstacles laid out on the track. Fortune has decreed that a couple of the faster kids are on James' team and when he is tagged in as the final runner, he's closer to the front than the back. He takes off, little legs moving faster than I've seen before. A trickle of excitement goes through me. Jesus, he might win!

'Come on, James!' Debs and I yell as one.

He jumps over the bench cleanly and then makes it through the plastic hoop without mishap. He's still close to the front. Holy Jesus! Holy frig! He really, really might win!

'Come on, James! Keep going, buddy! You can do it!'

He's got a clear run to the line and I'm not sure I've ever seen him move quite so fast. I grab Debs' arm, my nails digging into her skin. He's got little more than ten yards to go when. . . when . . . Without warning, he slows down. Then he stops running and he begins to skip. Skipping along the grass, the way he does when we take him for a walk around the duck pond on a Sunday morning. There are some words stuck in my throat and I can't quite get them out.

Several other children run past James as he skips merrily and in a leisurely fashion across the finish line. Then he walks over to his teammates. I'm not sure if another kid has said something to him, because he quickly turns to look for Debs and myself, for the first time today searching for reassurance, his little face seeking our approval. Debs is cheering and clapping wildly. I step forward. I've plenty of experience in how this society can pressurise you into doing what other people expect rather than what you want; I know how much courage it takes to do your own thing. And it turns out my son innately understands this better than I do. I'm wearing a huge smile and I give him the thumbs-up. He grins back and holds up his little thumb in return.

Sports day is finished. Watching James across the field I can tell he's got plenty of energy left. But I'm shattered. Some of the mothers and fathers hang around to get a cup of coffee and have a chat but we move away from them. I wonder for a moment why I allowed myself to get so uptight about the sports day. I suppose it's because I feel that some sort of parental responsibility has been at stake today. I feel that I'm at a significant early stage in a process of sending my child off to run his own races in life. So much of what he'll experience from now on will be about competition, achieving results, trying to be the best. I'm aware that there will be plenty more races over the years and I'll always worry. And I won't always be there to cheer him on from the sidelines.

We parents have been told not to approach the children after the races, because they have to go back to class. But I can't help myself and awkwardly step over the rope which separates us. I go to the little bench; my son is surprised to see me and stands up. I give him a quick cuddle and a fist-bump.

'Well done, buddy,' I say, 'you were brilliant.'

He's still smiling as he responds. 'Oh Daddy, I told you – it doesn't matter where you finish, as long as you have fun.'

Being a parent means being there to teach my child. But sometimes I can learn from him as well.

Twenty-Eight

Putting the Pieces Back Together

August 2019

It's the middle of the day and I'm lying on top of the bed, curled up as if I'm a foetus in the womb. It's a defensive position which is not working. Fear is all over me like a rash. To be specific, I feel it in my chest and stomach – visceral spasms of anxiety which rise out of my gut and pour into my limbs. I watch my hands tremble. It's like I've taken a bad drug and I just can't get it out of my system.

I'm terrified that someone might call at the door, or phone me or send a text. I can hear my mobile buzzing in the next room and the noise unnerves me even more. I just can't deal with human contact right now. I'm not really capable of rational thought either – emotions of such intensity tend to crush any attempt at logic. But, as I bury my head in the pillow, there's the beginning of an effort to understand and the forming of a question – how have I ended up back here again?

It's been some time since I've suffered a serious mental health collapse – almost three years, in fact, since I left my job at the paper; and six years since I found myself in Ward 12. While I still face challenges every day, I've been enjoying a long period of relative stability and contentment. For more than a year I've felt my old confidence and authority creeping back. I've been able to take on more professional tasks and balance them with domestic duties, and actively enjoying the responsibilities of looking after James. I've been sleeping and eating properly and even found myself looking towards the future with hope. Making plans. Just this morning I was thinking it was going to be a very good day. But perhaps I was putting too much faith in my defences, and wrongly assuming that the road would always be straight and flat.

So, what happened? Well, it's difficult to say. Maybe it was simply the tone of voice of someone at the other end of the phone? Or a plan that did not turn out quite as I'd hoped? Possibly even just a change in the weather? The point is not the trigger, but the reaction. And how drastically out of proportion it is; how easily I can be destabilised. How the mud, which is sometimes thrown by life, which other people seem to be able to shake off without a second thought, can stick to me and burn deep into my skin. And it all falls apart from there, the old demons rushing back into the vacuum and filling me with terror, attacking again and again until soon I've got no idea what set them off in the first place. I just have to try to cope today, not to ask why.

I attempt to distract myself with work but the words on the flickering white computer screen are swimming and I can't find any order in them. And I feel worse when I'm sitting upright; the weight on my chest is like an ache that won't go away. The crippling anxiety sends dizzying, multiple thoughts spinning around the interior of my brain at a truly frightening speed. I feel out of control, and that I need to move elsewhere in the search for relief.

I try to make a coffee but this only reinforces the extent of the trembling in my hands as I pour the boiling water from the kettle. I can't bear to look at these hands, so I walk into the back yard. The house and garden are quiet; James is staying with family members for a few hours – ironically, a well-intentioned attempt to give me some peace and quiet to work. Toys are scattered in the little paved area at the back of our house. There's a brightly-coloured basketball and, at the top of a thick pole nearby, a plastic hoop – a set designed to help young children to learn the basics of the game. I lift the ball and begin to bounce it on the hard tiles. There's something pleasing in the hollow, repetitive smack of plastic on stone. Then I throw it towards the hoop. I miss. I recover the ball and try again. Once more, I miss. My shaking hands are not helping but soon I've got myself into a rhythm of throwing. And missing.

I invent a game where I challenge myself to get better. I take ten throws and see how many times I can score a basket. Three at first, then four, then six and eventually seven. I try for what seems like a long time, but seven seems to be my limit. I'm certainly not Michael Jordan but as I line up each throw, the outcome takes on an importance in my mind beyond that of an NBA championship. It begins to rain but I keep going until the drops of precipitation are mixed with my perspiration. Hundreds of times, I take the little plastic ball and hurl it towards the hoop. Until eventually I score eight and, rather pathetically, in the rain and in the middle of a sea of toys, I clench my fist and let out a deep gasp of satisfaction.

I go back inside, noticing for the first time that the tremble in my hands has disappeared. But I'm not naive enough to think I've been able to cure myself with a game of basketball. Within minutes I can feel the anxiety beginning to return, like a persistent crow which won't leave the crops alone. I know from my experience that an episode like this may take several days to pass.

Then I have to go to pick up James. With him I have to

use every part of my knowledge and guile to disguise the fact that there is anything wrong, determined as I am to keep my inadequacies hidden. We play an imaginary, improvised game where he is a superhero and I'm a villain. This ends with James repeatedly banging me over the head with a foam replica of Thor's hammer. It's such a clunky metaphor for the day I'm enduring that I start laughing, each thump on the skull pushing me further into a state of helpless mirth. Soon it's time to make dinner and I force myself to concentrate on the task.

Debs comes home from work. I've already told her I'm suffering and she brings me a little present – a turquoise armband bearing the word 'Hope' in white letters. It's a distraction tactic, something to remind me that there's always a better day coming soon. It also works by providing comforting evidence of the fact that there are people who care about me. Of course, the armband will not change my life – nor will playing a basketball game in the rain or getting thumped on the head by Thor's hammer. But together they are just about enough to get me through the day.

In the evening, the blanket of anxiety is still over me, making it difficult to concentrate on the TV or to unwind and slow my breathing enough to be able to sleep. I'll have to accept that it will probably be like this for a while. And then it will pass and I'll return to my place of contentment, wondering why I allowed myself to get into such a state in the first place. I've been through it before and come out the other side. That's just the way it is, and in this battle, there's no room for complacency

So I do what I usually do – which is to write about it. Not as some sort of cry for help or to present myself as a worthy subject for pity. But rather because that's just what

I do – whether it's a good day or bad, trying to meet it face-to-face with the same level of honesty. Indeed, that's the point of this book – striving to make sense out of all the confusion and mess. I'm a lot better equipped to cope than I was when I was admitted to Ward 12 six years ago. Now the good days outnumber the bad. But when the bad ones come, I meet them head on and do whatever I have to do to cope. So, while it's my brain that lands me in this position, it's the same brain that I'll use to get me out of it again. And, of course, I have my wife and son to help me.

***

We're on the sea, somewhere just off the northern coast of Ireland, between the County Antrim town of Ballycastle and Rathlin island, when the weather changes. I can't identify a definite point when this happens; the alteration is so natural and seamless. At one point the waters are calm and we're congratulating ourselves on the wise decision to wear shorts and T-shirts for the boat trip, and then soon after it's windy and cold, and we're pulling on jumpers and fleeing from the exposed upper deck of the little ferry, wondering what happened.

We arrive on Rathlin, the only inhabited island off the coast of Northern Ireland and one of my favourite locations. We head straight for the play park. Debs and I take turns pushing James high on the swings. Then I rock the seesaw fast so that he's half-delighted, half-terrified. While he's moving up and down haphazardly, he yelps, 'Daddy, stop! I'm scared', but as soon as the movement ceases, he pleads for me to do it again.

It reminds me how fickle fear can be, and I think briefly about the anxiety I've been suffering. It's been six days since I suffered the major panic attack, and, like oil on water, the remnants of it have proven hard to shift. I'm a bit better today, otherwise I wouldn't even be able to countenance a family outing. There is still some anxiety nesting in my chest, but I've got it under some sort of control. I never pretend to have all, or even any, of the answers but I know that a day out in a place I love with the people I love seems to give me as good a chance of some peace as anything.

And here we are on Rathlin, just for a few hours, so we try to do lots of things in the short time we have. A spell in the park; a walk on the rocky beach with the grey sand and the rusty anchor; a dander along the narrow road which winds up the hill away from the bay. The island is a curious mix of the old and new, the charm of a community cut off from society alongside the recent efforts to maximise the tourism potential of the site. These days, you'll see rotting wooden fishing boats alongside brightly coloured jet-skis. There is much new development on the island but there are also ancient cars and tractors parked near the port, covered with a layer of light dust, which seemingly haven't been disturbed in years. It's the only place where I've seen a car with a floral window box attached to its door, the contents growing happily.

There are rotund, lazy seals lying stretched out near the port. A small cafe sells very bad coffee, compensated for by very good cake. There's an abundance of sea and land birds. We've been told that the rare, nostalgic call of the corncrake has recently been heard once more on the island, although we realise that the shy bird is hardly likely to put in an appearance while James is noisily snapping around my heels complaining that his legs are tired, and begging to be lifted.

Like I said, we squeeze a lot into a short period of time and there's a pleasing weariness in our limbs as we sit on a large rock and wait for the ferry to slide into the harbour to bring us back to the Irish mainland. When you watch the ferry at sea from afar, it seems barely to be moving at all. And today I'm in no rush.

As I sit there on the dark rock, it occurs to me that my anxiety has gone. For the first time in six days, I become aware that the spasms of tension coursing from my stomach to my chest have stopped. I'm completely relaxed and content. For now, anyway. I try to think about it, to recollect the exact moment when the fear left me and the world seemed to become benign once more. But I can't. It's so gradual and subliminal that the shift in me happened without being noticed, just like the earlier change in the weather on the stretch of water between Ballycastle and Rathlin.

Twenty-Nine

Lockdown

May 2020

It is the morning of a working day and I'm in a meeting.

But, instead of gathering around a table with colleagues, I am in my kitchen while their faces are staring at me from a computer screen. Halfway through, my son enters the room and tries to sit on my knee. I indulge him for a bit, gently stroking his golden hair, before I have to ease him back into the hallway. There are subjects being discussed at this meeting that no seven-year-old should have to hear. This is the new normal.

***

It was just a couple of months ago that, once again, my life moved in an unexpected direction. A chance meeting led to me receiving an offer to return to full-time work. The proposed job was in a daily newspaper. I was unwilling at first, unsure if the scars from the last time had been given enough time to heal. But I talked it over with Debs and there was a lot about the opportunity which seemed to make sense. First of all, James, now in P3, is settled in his education. He is becoming more confident, with his own circle of friends. The truth is that he doesn't need me in the way that he once did.

Secondly, we agreed that I had been restored enough to be sufficiently robust to deal with the challenge of being back in a newsroom; in fact, we thought, it might even help me. One of the main issues I have been dealing with for some time is the long hours of boredom while my son is in school. I needed a diversion. The third and most compelling argument was finance. Four years of being a part-time stay-at-home dad with only limited income had begun to bite sharply. Where before my sleepless nights may have been caused by executive stress, more recently the long night-time hours were filled for me with fretting over how we were going to pay all the bills.

And so, with much uncertainty, I accepted the newspaper job. However, I was clear that things had to be different from the last time around. I told my new bosses that I would arrive at and leave the office at a certain time every day, and that there'd be no phone calls taken at home. Also, and most importantly, I vowed to myself that I would not allow my new role to dictate my life – I would try my best to help, but there was only so much of myself I was prepared to expose to the job. Once these things had been determined, I slipped once more into the routine of office work, confident that I had built my defences high, and that I would be able to spot danger from whatever direction it galloped. Wrongly, as it turned out, I assumed that I would see it coming.

I had been in the position for just a few weeks when the first reports about coronavirus made it into the paper. Soon, as the infection spread across the world, it began to dominate all the news pages and all of our lives. First the schools were closed and then, as we moved into full lockdown, the office where I worked. While it was of course not new for me to be working from home, I was now doing it full-time while combining it with the roles of parent and teacher – Debs' responsibilities as a broadcast journalist meant that she still had to work away from the house a lot. Previously, even when I was at my lowest point, there had always been some degree of separation between these parts of my life; now, they had been meshed together into some sort of untidy pulp. There was no longer a defined start or an end to the working day. The computer was always there on the kitchen table, the screen blinking provocatively at me; I was also always with my son.

***

By now it is the middle of the working day and I am trying to do some schoolwork with James. It seems to be a task I am temperamentally unsuited for. We complete a few of the worksheets that the school has sent home before I abandon it, unsure if any meaningful progress has been made. So far today we have played in the garden, gone for a little walk, done some reading and shared lunch – all while I've been trying to further the completion of tomorrow's newspaper.

I have a low feeling, one that is borne of a suspicion that this new arrangement means I'm not doing anything well enough, since I'm unable to give my full attention to either my job or my newly revisited role as a stay-at-home father. There is also the recognition that the world, for my son, is not as it should be. He has beloved school friends, cousins, aunts, uncles and grandparents, but now he has been suddenly ripped away from direct contact with all of them. What was once routine is now forbidden, as we are restricted to the four walls of our house. We have only one child; there is no brother or sister for James to play with. There is no park or play facility open to which I can take him. At a time when his personality and curiosity is blossoming apace, he's been deprived of the social interaction and new experiences which would nourish his development.

Throughout it all James has been wonderful, accepting with a maturity beyond his years that all is not as it was, and that sacrifices have to be made. However desperate he is to play with his friends and cousins, he does not complain. But he's also a seven-year-old boy with a voracious appetite for fun, learning and adventure. It is natural that he will come to me often, wanting to me to play or just be with him. Sometimes I take him outside, watching him laugh with abandon as he races on his scooter; sometimes he just sits beside me, drawing pictures or inventing stories as I type on the computer.

Work has to be done. I try to find a balance between these conflicting demands, but it is inevitable that one thing bleeds into the other. Now, when my son asks me to play with him, he always precedes it with, 'Just if you have time, Daddy. . .' Every time I hear that I can't help feeling a little bit more diminished as a father, even though I know, and remind myself, that this situation is not of my making.

It is late in the afternoon now and I'm falling behind where I need to be with the daily tasks. The production of a newspaper depends on maintaining a steady pace, where enough things are being done at certain times to keep the whole rusty old vehicle trundling along. But I'm not moving quickly enough and I'm left with no option but to lead James into the front room. I put a film on the TV and leave him some snacks. I ruffle his hair and tell him I'll be in the next room, and that I'll check on him every few minutes.

I continue working in the kitchen. After a while I

notice that there is no sound coming from the television. I go to check. James is sitting on the floor playing a game. It's a board game we bought him with counters and dice. He is playing it by himself, pretending there are two people. He takes one turn with the dice and then moves around to the other side of the board and takes the other. He is having a conversation with himself as he does this.

He has his back to me as I watch, which is welcome, because at that moment something splinters inside me. I walk back to the kitchen and the tears finally come, like a yolk bursting open. Perhaps I'm crying for my son; perhaps it is for everyone who is suffering; perhaps it is just for myself. I wash my face at the kitchen sink, chastising myself for my weakness and selfishness. The tears are wasted, because there is nothing else to do but get on with things. I go back into the other room. My son looks up at me hopefully.

'Just if you have time, Daddy, would you be able to play with me?'

I sit on the floor beside him and pick up the dice, putting my other arm around him.

'Of course I will, buddy. Of course I will.'

***

It is early in the evening of the same day. Debs is now home from work and is putting James to bed. I step into the back garden to drink in the last drops of warm air before the night-time chill descends. I take a seat in my old familiar spot. I sit there for some time, my mind barren.

I look around, trying to take my perspective outside of my own thoughts. There are colours in the garden – ochre, pale yellow, startling pink, and varying depths of green.

I'm no gardener and I'm struck by how this cycle continues without any interference or direction from me. While some buds have sprouted already, others remain just a promise. Plants, like people, develop at their own pace.

I realise there is something even more diverting than the wash of the leaves: it is the sound. Or rather, the lack of it. The air is still tonight so there is no rustle from the tips of the tree branches. The birdsong has long since quietened. Even more noticeably, there is no low thunder of traffic from the nearby road, no distant rumble of a plane in the sky. There are no cries of children playing; no adults talking. There is no urgent rush of oil burners firing.

I have sat in this same spot countless evenings before – but I'm not sure I've ever noticed this vacuum of silence. Is it always this way, or is this another manifestation of our new situation? The silence is, at the same time, both reassuring and disconcerting. I enjoy the peace, but still like to hear some activity, just to remind me that there is something else out there, on the other side of the garden fence. I find myself crunching my feet on the loose stones, just to create a sound.

I think about the day which has just passed. It was a challenge, balancing work with parenting and education, and I had a good cry (as you may have noticed, I do this a lot). But while I'm worn out, I find that I feel a level of peace and contentment. One of the things that I have often been told over the years is that a critical warning signal when it comes to mental illness is reaching a point where you can't see a way out, when you have no hope for a better day. And so, even though the public health crisis and lockdown has created adversity for everyone, I'm encouraged that I am not experiencing a more profound darkness in a personal sense.

Tomorrow is Saturday. The three of us will share breakfast and dinner at the same table, play together, watch a film, go for a walk. James will talk a lot, and Debs and I will listen. Later, when he is dreaming, my wife and I will watch something silly on TV. She will have a glass of wine while I munch crisps. There is nothing else that we are allowed to do and there is an undoubted degree of attraction in this slower pace of life.

Lockdown has brought strain to me and others. But while that is true, it is only honest to state that it is not the full picture. The restrictions have also created a more profound sense of appreciation of, and keener ability to distinguish between, what is truly important in my life and what I can do without.

I think about what I miss most about the old normal. Above all, it's being able to see extended family and friends, and watching my son playing with those of his own age. Beyond that, many things now seem dispensable. My whole life has been lived believing sport to be more important than it really is. Now that most spectator sports have been suspended, I find I don't think much about them. The new reality has separated the substance from the garnish.

I consider how a normal weekend day, before the pandemic, would have looked. There would have been a panicked attempt to squeeze in many activities. We would have tried to take James to a class or play date in the morning; spent the afternoon fighting our way around a supermarket or clothes shop; visited people for some forced small talk; perhaps gone out for dinner in the evening. All while I'd be trying to keep up with the progress of multiple sporting events on my phone and checking social media. The frenzied pace of life meant there was a constant anxiety about the next thing that needed to be done, and the thing after that, and not enough focus on what is in front of our eyes.

I feel a level of guilt that I am finding positives in the middle of a pandemic – a deadly contagion whose claws are so long and pointed that the agony being suffered by many is absolute. But the crisis must eventually pass and then, for those of us who are lucky enough to still be here, some of the things that enrich and colour our lives will start up again. Perhaps we will be just as we were before; or perhaps, because the trauma has the potential to change us, we will be slightly altered. The upsurge in kindness and compassion throughout communities which has become apparent during this crisis will hopefully prove to be more enduring than the virus which spawned it.

The air is cooler now and I'm surprised at how long I've been sitting in the same spot. It is harder to see the plants in the now failing light. I enjoy the peace for a few more moments before I go back inside. One of the many effects of the lockdown has been to sharpen my senses towards what is around me. Beyond this, it has given me the chance to have precious time with my wife and son that I would otherwise have missed. Distractions have been removed as the social restrictions mean I have settled into a calmer, purer set of habits.

Tomorrow will be a family day. We have nothing in particular to do and nowhere that we need (or are allowed) to go to. It will be just the three of us in our home. I'm looking forward to it. When everything else is taken away, what is left is what is most important. And, as I constantly remind myself, it's all I've ever really needed.

Epilogue

The Same Place

'I'm glad you're in a better place now.'

That's a statement I've heard and read countless times in the past few years. It's true that if you hear or see the same words over and over again, they eventually lose any proper meaning in your mind. I'm partly to blame, no doubt. I've certainly assisted people in forming the simplistic view that everything's fine when the truth is a little more complicated than that. When well-meaning people keep asking you how you're doing, then you get used to using empty cliché as a diversionary tactic. I mean, what's the alternative? 'Actually, I was having some suicidal thoughts just before you dropped round. Now, do you want a chocolate biscuit with your tea?'

I don't think most people want that much honesty. Everybody praises the bravery of speaking out – but what they really want to hear is that there's a happy ending. That you've beaten it. No messy loose ends, please. But here's my truth. There is no 'better place'. I can no more stop the workings of my mind than teach my hair to grow shorter. The terror is still there. Every day. The raven of despair still constantly hovers close by. The dark thoughts are as inevitable as a Monday morning. On my very best days, at the happiest times of my life, I can still have life-ending thoughts. Maybe up to one hundred times a day.

Does that sound incessantly bleak? Well, it needn't. Because that's the breakthrough. That's the realisation that perhaps has saved me. Simply accepting that is the way my mind works has finally given me what I'd been searching for all of my life: a little bit of peace. For as long as I can remember I'd always assumed I'd get to an age where everything would make sense. When all the edges of the shifting tectonic plates would rub together smoothly. When, perhaps at 20, at 30, at 40 – at some stage anyway – I would reach a point where I'd have beaten my own monsters. A time when my mind would be tamed. When I would just feel security and happiness. I would get off the pills forever; I'd never have to be afraid again. I'd finally be rid of the maggot worthlessness that has always infested my soul.

But it just never seemed to happen. Not only that, but as the years passed by, things clearly got worse. The more successful I was at work, the more chaotic my inner world became. Then came the breakdowns; the occasions when I came close to suicide; the time in hospital. I'd had to leave my job. I'd had enough. I had no idea what I was going to do with the rest of my life. I had no idea if there was going to be a rest of my life. I was tired. Just tired. So tired of fighting against my own mind.

So I stopped. There was no decision made to do it. No convenient moment of clarity or discernible turning point that I can relate as a neat story around which to build this conclusion. I can only suppose that the fact of being away from the pressure of work must have helped me relax a little in the first instance. Freedom, for the first time in 20 years, from the unrelenting routine of deadlines and the next edition allowed my shattered nerves to begin to heal.

Because of work I'd missed James' first week of nursery school. Now I was free of it, and able to help him as he struggled to adapt to the new environment. I was able to be there for him. To be with him in the mornings, helping him have his breakfast, fighting over the ritual of getting dressed. I was there to hold his hand as we went to the school door, to talk calmly to him as he wept and pleaded to be allowed to go back home; to hug him and wave goodbye. When it was home time, I was there, standing among all the mummies. I'd usually see him before he saw me; I'd watch as, looking initially uncertain and anxious, he'd spot me and start to run, his bottom lip trembling as he jumped into my arms.

Soon I began to enjoy it. I became familiar with all the drop-off and pick-up times. I learnt the names of all his classmates and made friends with their parents. I was there for the school trip, the nativity play, the school disco, the Spring fair, the Open Day, the Sports Day. I always tried to be the daddy who played with all the kids, the first one in the bouncy castle. I made a cake for my son's birthday party; I learnt how to make balloon animals. We enjoyed lots of time together as a family. Debs, James and me.

People told me I looked better. I gained some weight; grew a terrible beard; became easier to talk to, less serious. I entered the Santa Run in the village where I live. The look of joy on my boy's face as he stood by my side when I was presented with my second-place medal was memorable.

So, had I been healed by a few years away from work?

Absolutely not. All of the old problems and fears still remained. I remember one day being in a shop with my wife, and suffering such a severe panic attack that she had to rush me straight home. But the strange thing was, it didn't seem to bother me so much anymore. I didn't allow getting down to get me down. I tried to accept the nasty thoughts which buzzed around in my head as part of me. When I had a low period, I just waited for it to pass. I stopped battling against my own mind. Instead, I accepted it. This is me. It's the way my brain is. I stopped being so hard on myself. I'd found what balanced me out against the worst excesses of myself. Just a little bit of contentment.

I'd done all the treatments. The medication, the counselling, the meditation. But simply having fun took me a lot further. Learning to smile, to laugh, to play. My son gave that back to me. Everyone who suffers is different. We all just have to find what works best for each of us.

I lived the life of the stay-at-home daddy as I tried to figure out what to do with myself. I loved being a full-time parent but there was still a part of me which needed a creative outlet. There were moments when I felt cut off from the world. Isolated. I needed stimulation, just like my son. I played around with the idea of doing some writing. But nothing ever seemed to work out; I could never seem to make an idea stick. I launched a blog. Then I spoke publicly about mental health. Then I wrote this book. Once I got over the first hurdle of telling people about my suffering, of accepting that this would be my label from now on, it all got a lot easier.

As I began this new journey, I also started to discover the process of writing for therapy. It worked like this. I've always found it easier to express my ideas through stories. Often thoughts which don't make sense internally achieve a logic when they're committed as part of a narrative. I found aspects of my own struggle seemed to lose part of their terror when I wrote about them. Then there was the power of solidarity, of networking. Of discovering that thoughts and fears which I had always assumed were peculiar to me were actually common, even universal. I was able to experience the wonderful warm feeling of support from others.

It feels good to be part of something creative again. It's exciting and fun, and it helps me. But still, I don't have any sense of complacency about my own mental health. I never know when the next bad day is coming. The next breakdown. The next collapse. None of us do. But I do feel that if it comes, I'm better equipped than ever to cope. I've got my family. My writing. My smile. Once you accept the internal terror, then it doesn't seem to be quite as scary anymore. I'll always be afraid of the dark, but I just have to keep reminding myself that the sun rises again a few hours later. So, to bring it back to where I started this chapter – I'm not in a better place, I'm in the same place. But I'm learning to love that place. I'm learning to be kinder to myself.

***

When I was close to finishing this book, I was contacted by a group of mothers who run an online parenting forum. They were putting together a series from writers penning letters to their 'pre-parent' selves, and asked me to contribute. I loved the idea immediately. It seemed like a perfect way to condense everything that I've spent the last few years writing about into one short missive. It would also serve as a reminder that, while it is wonderful when other people read my words, the most important audience will always be myself.

So I entered into the challenge and thought earnestly about what I should write if the recipient was a younger version of myself; the version of myself who was simply not equipped to deal with the challenges presented by my own brain. What would I most want to hear? What might bring some comfort to a troubled mind? I thought about the boy who was once tied to the seat on the school bus; about the teenager who was humiliated by the family GP. I thought about the young man who suffered miserably at work but kept going for years because he knew no other way. I thought about being locked up in a hospital ward and a nurse shining a torch in my face to make sure I was still alive. I thought about standing on motorway bridges, at the edge of cliffs, about locking myself into toilets and days when I could not find the strength to get out of bed. Then I thought of my family, my wife and son. And I began to cry. Then I steadied myself and started to type.

Dear Jonny –

Knowing you as I do, I'm sure you will be rather chuffed to receive a written letter. It may be hard to imagine, but this form of communication will become rare in your future years. It is all instant and impersonal these days – texts, emails and social media. I've no doubt you would love me to tell you that you will get the hang of it all, but we both know what you are like with technology.

I imagine you will have many questions about me and that's ok. I don't have time here to answer them all now but maybe we could keep talking and work it all out as we go? I'd like that a lot. I will settle now for telling you that I've been asked to write this letter because I do a bit of 'blogging' these days. I know you won't yet understand what that means and, even if I explained it, you wouldn't believe it.

Of course, the first question is, which younger version of Jonny should I be addressing this letter to? Should it be the scared kid who used wit and humour to cover up crippling fear? The successful journalist who lost his way in a ruthless profession? No. I'm thinking of the day when you, the younger Jonny, might need a letter from me the most. That day when you just couldn't see the point anymore and decided it was too hard to go on. I don't need to go into specifics – we both know the day I'm talking about.

Now I suppose you are hoping that I will tell you that it's all going to be ok. That it gets easier. That you work it all out at some point and reach that place of serenity and peace that you have always dreamed about. The problem is Jonny, and I'm actually crying for you as I write this, it doesn't. The truth is that it will always be this hard for you. The fear and anxiety, the suffocation of depression will always be there. I'm so sorry to have to tell you this, but that's just the way your mind works.

And I'm sorry for another reason too. I'm sorry that I didn't know back then how to be kinder to you, or have any useful way of helping you. Sorry that I was so hard on you all the time. I'm afraid I just didn't know how to love you and that will always be my deepest regret.

But there is something else that I really want you to know. And this is that someday you will have a family all of your own. You will meet a wonderful girl and get married. It will take a lot of time but you will eventually admit to her what goes on in your head. And guess what? She will still love you anyway and you will realise how many years were wasted, keeping it all wrapped up.

And then there is your future son – the other main reason I am writing to you today. Your beautiful boy, who will change everything the first time you hold his writhing little body in your arms and he peers angrily at you. Get used to that look: you are going to see a lot more of it over the years! You and he will learn together and both stumble repeatedly along the way. At times you will be crushed by the awe-inspiring responsibility of trying to raise and shape another human being. In some ways it will take you still further away from normal society because you will never quite shake that early wide-eyed amazement of what you are doing. You'll never lose that desire to go up to total strangers in the street, grab them and yell, 'Look at my son! Isn't he just wonderful?' When people ask you what you do, your first answer will always be the same – 'I'm a father'.

But there will be many more bad days. I'm afraid to tell you this but some of them will be worse than you have yet known. The biggest challenges are still to come. But here is the thing you really need to remember. When they come, you will have your family to help you through them. When it is really bad, you will not be alone. When the night is at its deepest, there will be three in the bed and there will always be loving arms stretching out to hold you in the dark. I suppose it is what you and I have always been searching for. A reason for it all. It is a place which feels like home.

You will also learn that there is no universal path or method which leads away from despair and towards contentment. There are many different ways of finding refuge in this battle and each person has to find out what works best for them as individuals. When it comes to dealing with mental illness, the closest thing to an absolute truth you will discover is the undeniable power and benefit of talking about it, and how much lighter the burden will feel when you share it with another. In your own way, by choosing to write and talk about your story publicly, you will perhaps play a tiny part in helping to dispel the stigma which hinders recovery for so many. I hope you will agree that is a pretty good reason to stay alive.

The problem with writing letters is knowing how to finish; how to find a neat way of summing up all that has gone before. But how about this? You will have a family that you love. They will also love you. But more importantly, because of them, you will learn to love yourself.

Take care, Jonny. I love you so much. I'm sorry it took me so many years to say it.

******

Acknowledgements

Primarily I wish to thank my agents and publishers, Susan and Paul Feldstein, for making this book a reality. Without Susan's patience, persistence and knowledge, this would all have remained just another idea rattling around in my brain.

I am deeply grateful to the Arts Council of Northern Ireland for their invaluable financial assistance with this project.

A number of people agreed to read or review this book prior to publication and I am indebted to them all, including Gareth O'Callaghan, Dearbhail McDonald, Frank Mitchell, Lindsay Robinson, Peter Cardwell, Sam McBride, Alex Kane and Suzanne Breen.

My deepest thanks go to the staff who looked after me on Ward 12, and all of the doctors, nurses, counsellors and psychiatrists who have treated me since.

My deepest apologies to all of the work colleagues who have had to put up with me.

A final word of appreciation to my family, both extended and immediate, for their unfailing support. My love goes to Debs and James, who gave me the strength to keep going when I feared I could not.

Printed in Great Britain
by Amazon

60556156R00156